Crosscurrents / MODERN CRITIQUES

Harry T. Moore, *General Editor*

HENRY
DE MONTHERLANT
A Critical Biography

Lucille Becker

WITH A PREFACE BY
Harry T. Moore

SOUTHERN ILLINOIS UNIVERSITY PRESS
Carbondale and Edwardsville

FEFFER & SIMONS, INC.
London and Amsterdam

147651

Contents

Preface

Professor Lucille Becker has performed a useful service indeed in providing us with so thorough a critical biography of Henry de Montherlant, an important French writer who is too little known in this country. As Professor Becker points out, Montherlant's most significant contribution has been to the theater, though his plays are hardly ever performed over here. I remember, a few years ago, a very fine performance, on the National Educational Television network, of Le Maître de Santiago (as of course The Master of Santiago, a British production); but otherwise I have never had the chance, in America, of seeing a Montherlant play. Fortunately, Alfred Knopf has given American publication to The Master of Santiago and Four Other Plays, so that readers at least have a chance to become acquainted with Montherlant as a playwright, which the present book may induce them to do.

As a novelist, Montherlant has fared somewhat better in English-speaking countries and, whether or not his fiction is widely read, it is at least available. The novel usually considered to be his finest, Les Célibataires, has had at least three translations, as The Bachelors, as Lament for the Death of an Upper Class, and as Perish in Their Pride. His fiction has been more regularly printed in England than in the United States.

Montherlant has, because of his concern with sports in his writings, sometimes been compared with Hemingway, but they are writers who are worlds apart. Montherlant's work is complicated beyond any possible similarity to Hemingway. And in the present book, Professor Becker investigates the pervasive complexity of the French author. She shows, for example, how the structure of the bullfight is related to the structure of some of his dramas, a feature not found in Hemingway; and she further shows how these dramas yet have an essentially classical structure.

She also deals thoroughly with the philosophical side of Montherlant, with such elements of his temperament as his nihilism and his irony. Further, Professor Becker calls attention to the essential solitude of Montherlant's characters: "Each of [his] dramas embodies the search for human comprehension and demonstrates its impossibility."

The series Crosscurrents/Modern Critiques has published a number of books on modern French literature. Professor Becker's is an imposing addition to the list. In its investigation of Henry de Montherlant's life, thought, and writing technique, it has much to say that will interest students of French literature; and it is a book which, for those not too well acquainted with the subject, effectively introduces a highly significant author.

HARRY T. MOORE

Southern Illinois University
May 1, 1969

Introduction

Since the publication of his first book in 1920, Henry de Montherlant has occupied a preeminent position in French letters as a novelist, essayist, poet, and dramatist. Georges Bernanos acclaimed him as "possibly the greatest of our living writers," [1] even before his plays, his greatest literary achievement, had been written. He has been described as "perhaps the only dramatist since Racine and Corneille worthy of ranking with them," [2] and as "the greatest living French prose writer." [3] In a survey conducted by the literary weekly *Carrefour*, Montherlant was voted the contemporary French writer who would be most read in the year 2000. To this acclaim was added his election to membership in the French Academy on March 25, 1960.

The critical recognition accorded to Montherlant is particularly significant since his work, in large measure, remains outside the mainstream of contemporary French literature. His glorification of the exceptional exploits and moral superiority of the hero is aristocratic, in a day when the literature of that class has died out. While the majority of modern authors are preoccupied with the problems of their time, Montherlant, in conformity with the great classical tradition, is concerned with the eternal problems of the human soul. His emphasis on stylistic perfection is in contrast to the indifference of so many contemporary authors, for whom language is only a means used to transmit their ideas.

Despite those qualities that set it apart, Montherlant's work indelibly bears the mark of the twentieth century. The heroism and nobility extolled by him are merely his answer to the anguish felt by modern man in a universe deprived of all transcendent values. The search for a philosophy to guide man, at a time when all traditional systems have proved inadequate, has led Montherlant to adopt the two principles which provide the framework on which his work has been built. The first, the doctrine of "syncretism and alternation," is essentially optimistic as it asserts the fundamental goodness of all things in nature and the necessity for man to taste of every experience in order to find happiness. Life, in all of its manifestations, is a force which does not have to be justified, just lived to the fullest.

Although there are indications in Montherlant's early works of the pessimism and nihilism that govern the work of his later years, they reflect, as a whole, the basic *joie de vivre* of youth, which sees before it infinite possibilities for self-fulfillment. They transcribe the author's passion for life and his confidence in the joys it will afford him.

In his continued attempt to widen the field of his experiences, Montherlant, sated with what he had obtained and desperate for all that had eluded him, gradually began to believe that nothing had meaning and nothing was worthwhile. This belief led him to the second of his principles, that of "useless service," which provides the key to the works of his maturity and which postulates action in full knowledge of the uselessness of such action. Action without faith is the credo of the heroes of Montherlant's later works. These writings increasingly reflect the preoccupations of old age, and differ from Montherlant's early works by their overwhelming sadness. Montherlant's literary production thus may be divided into two groups, the works preceding and those following his forty-fifth birthday. The first group, including the autobiographical works as well as the novels and essays of his youth, reflect his search for ubiquity through alternation. The plays, notebooks, and the novel *Le Chaos et la Nuit*, of his later years, bear witness to the bitterness of useless service and the inexorable march toward death.

I am grateful to Editions Gillimard for its kind permission to quote from the works of Henry de Montherlant. All translations into English are mine.

LUCILLE BECKER

Drew University
March 1969

Henry de Montherlant
A Critical Biography

1

A Song of Life

Henry Millon de Montherlant was born in Paris on April 21, 1896. His father's family, which may have originated in Spain, had settled centuries before in Picardy on the northwestern coast of France. It is from his father that Montherlant inherited the serious, arrogant, somewhat taciturn side of his character. His belief in his Spanish ancestry may also account for the constant interest he has shown in that land of violent contrasts and extreme temperaments, which has provided the background for several of his novels and plays.[1] His mother, a granddaughter of Count Henry de Riancey, a nineteenth-century champion of the church and monarchy, transmitted to her son her zest for life and her gaiety. A strong influence was also exerted on Montherlant by his devout maternal grandmother, in whose home he lived until he was twenty-seven years old.

During the early years spent at the *écoles* Janson de Sailly and Saint-Pierre, in Neuilly, two important events occurred which influenced his artistic development. The first was his discovery of ancient Rome on reading Sienkiewicz's *Quo Vadis*. This book stimulated his interest in pagan antiquity with its love of beauty and frank sensuality. More than fifty years later, in the postface to his play, *La Guerre Civile*, Montherlant was to reveal the extent of this influence.

The Roman art of living stretched from the art of pleasure to the art of dying, with courage, gravity, infamy, and sadness between the two. That is why their history is a microcosm of all history. . . . I have lived for sixty years among these shadowy Roman figures, a ghost among ghosts. At times I have gone to them to seek a reason for exaltation, at times a model of conduct, and at times a way in which to react in difficult moments. Who has not had those moments when everything seems to disintegrate and when there is an urgent need to grasp hold of a railing? When that has happened to me, the railing has always been Roman history.[2]

The influence of his classical studies was to counterbalance the lessons of his Catholic upbringing, producing throughout his life and work a continual alternation between pagan sensuality and Christian asceticism.

The second important influence of these early years was his introduction to bullfighting in Bayonne in 1909. He later went to Spain to enter the ring, an experience which he transposed into the lyrical, autobiographical novel *Les Bestiaires*. The bullfight, a microcosm of all of man's existence, is the focal point of Montherlant's novel of 1963, *Le Chaos et la Nuit*.

Les Enfances de Montherlant, by his childhood friend J. N. Faure-Biguet, contains a great deal of valuable information about Montherlant's early years. He started to write at the age of six and, in 1905, collaborated with Faure-Biguet on a Roman novel entitled *Pro una terra*. His biographer also mentions a story called "Love," written by Montherlant when he was thirteen years old, which is significant as a forerunner of his novel *Les Jeunes Filles*. The story takes place in Russia. In a troika which is crossing the steppes, two young newlyweds are exchanging kisses and tender words. Suddenly, they find themselves pursued by wolves and will be overtaken unless the load in the troika is lightened. The man throws his bride to the ground and makes his escape while the wolves devour her.

In 1911, Montherlant entered the *collège* Sainte-Croix de Neuilly to prepare for his *baccalauréat*. Together with a few of his friends, he formed a secret society, the members of which were united by solemn oaths of fidelity. Upon the discovery of this "order," the school authorities, alarmed by Montherlant's influence on the other boys, dissolved the organization and expelled him. The memory of his expulsion has remained with him throughout his life and has contributed in no small measure to the constant feeling of solitude and exile expressed in his work. Montherlant's experiences at Sainte-Croix de Neuilly inspired the essays of *La Relève du matin*, published at the author's expense in 1920, the play *La Ville dont le Prince est un enfant* (1951), and the novel *Les Garçons* (1969).

The essays of *La Relève du matin* were written between 1914 and 1918. Although Montherlant has since criticized certain youthful excesses of style, many important themes which recur throughout his work make their first appearance here. The book glorifies the Catholic *collège* and its salutary influence on the students.

It is also in this work that Montherlant's predilection for adolescence is first expressed. The work opens with a dialogue between the author and a priest as they watch the latter's students play ball one fall afternoon. When the priest exclaims that the boys seem to exhale an air of Christianity, the author replies that they are divinely inspired. Dissatisfied with the world around them, they are drawn towards God, driven by a "passion for knowledge, by a desire for sacrifice, by tenderness, by dreams of glory." [3] At thirteen, the young boy enters into the moment of his greatest glory, before he is forced to make the choices that will govern the rest of his life. Before their flame is extinguished, states the author, the priests should create premature crises in certain chosen souls, provoking the suffering that will hasten the awakening of the intelligence.

The essay entitled, "La Gloire du collège," is dedicated to the generation that died with only their memories of the *collège* behind them, for the collegians of Montherlant's generation went directly from school to the front. Of all those in Montherlant's class who had gone to war, only he survived. The message Montherlant preached here was to reappear many times in his work. He admonished his countrymen to become strong and to acquire a taste for force so that, in the future, they would not have to gather to honor new dead.

The years from 1912 to 1914, Montherlant's "worldly period," have been described by him as years of absolute mediocrity. His frequentation of society confirmed his distaste for the hypocrisy and banality of bourgeois existence. In 1914, he discovered that one of his dearest friends, a former member of the secret society at Sainte-Croix, was leaving for the front. He asked his mother for permission to enlist in the army but, because she knew that she was dying, she begged her son to remain behind. Although he acceded to her wish, he expressed his resentment in a play, *L'Exil*. His mother died shortly after he had completed the play, and Montherlant decided to withhold publication out of respect for her memory. As a result, *L'Exil* was not published until 1929.

This play, a few dramatic dialogues which are included in *La Relève du matin*, and the dramatic poem *Pasiphaé*, have caused Montherlant to be characterized as a dramatist who very early deviated from his course to become an essayist and a novelist. It was not until 1941 that Montherlant returned to the theater to write the plays that constitute his major literary contribution. Despite its autobiographical nature, *L'Exil* will be discussed with Montherlant's other plays which it resembles in content as well as form.

After the death of his mother, Montherlant enlisted in the army, refusing a commission. Although assigned to limited service for reasons of ill health, he requested active duty, in the course of which he was seriously wounded. After his release from the hospital, he became an interpreter for the American army and remained with them until he was demobilized in September, 1919. Montherlant's war experiences are recounted in the autobiographical novel *Le Songe*, published in 1922, which deals with the adventures at the front of the hero, Alban de Bricoule.

Alban, like the author, is assigned to inactive duty for physical reasons, but his nature will not permit him to remain behind. His decision to enlist is prompted both by his desire to rejoin his school friend, Prinet, and also to achieve peace of mind through violent action. Before leaving to join the "holy virile order," [4] Alban takes leave of the two women who are the prototypes of all of the women in Montherlant's later work. Dominique Soubrier, the young athlete, represents the virile, intelligent woman, with whom communication, even friendship, is possible. Douce, Alban's mistress with the allegorical name, belongs to the group of women men take in their arms,[5] the passive, unthinking objects who exist only for the pleasure of the hero.

Alban is intoxicated with the idea of joining the army, where things occupy the places and ranks they deserve according to the laws of reason. He is prepared to die, if necessary, since here he will die in a manner of which he approves. The danger he seeks provides him with a marvelous exaltation, the menace of death awakens his sensuality. When he has killed his first German, he feels an increase in virility, he has fulfilled the tribal rite for initiation into manhood. Yet he feels pity for the dying German prisoners and notes how much alike are all men when confronted with death. Montherlant paints the suffering of the prisoners in bitter detail to the last anguished cry of one who begs Alban to remain beside him so that he will not die alone.

The struggle between humanity and inhumanity is repeated over and over again throughout the novel. It is reflected in the dialogue which takes place within Alban, in which one voice assures him that this life is the one that suits his nature, while the other answers that what is happening there is abominable, that nothing excuses the senseless butchery. "The two thoughts fought like two eagles at the summit of space, and they turned and they sent forth terrible cries, and black feathers fell, and they loved each other while they fought." [6]

Although Alban is prepared to die in battle, or give his life for his friend, Prinet, he does not believe in the cause, or even in the friendship, for which he would be sacrificing himself. He explains this paradox in terms of a game he plays with life:

> I am unaware of the purpose of my sacrifice, and fundamentally I believe that I sacrifice myself to something that is nothing but one of those chimeras I hate. Believing my sacrifice to be useless, and perhaps mad, without a witness and without desire, renouncing life and the dear smell of living beings, I throw myself into the indifference of the future, proud at having been so free. . . . Thus have I lived, knowing the vanity of things, but acting as if I were deceived, and playing at being a man so that I would not be rejected as a god.[7]

The sham which he describes as the basis for all of his actions is the essence of "useless service," one of the unchanging tenets of Montherlant's philosophy.

Prinet is disturbed by his friend's cynicism, but Alban swears that he will never abandon his comrade. Nevertheless, they separate after a quarrel and Prinet is killed. After his death, Alban realizes that life has meaning not in terms of abstractions, but only in terms of human relationships. The war no longer interests him without the presence of his friend. With Prinet at his side, he had accepted the futility of his actions, but now everything became empty of meaning.

> The misery that was bearable yesterday because the other was experiencing it at the same time as he, became odious. There was no longer any sweetness in suffering. There was no longer that silent esteem, as warm as another's hand on your own.[8]

In the absence of Prinet, he becomes afraid of an obscure, unattended death, a wasted death without a witness, and leaves the front.

When he reaches the rear lines, Alban again meets Dominique, who has become an army nurse. Their former rapport is destroyed by the passion she now feels for him. For Alban, Dominique had represented an ideal much rarer than physical pleasure. Now he feels that she has degraded herself and broken the pact of friendship that had joined them. Realizing that he had been wrong to consider her an equal, he rejects her and returns to the purity of the war.

To those who objected to his glorification of war, Montherlant replied that it was the desire to suffer, to love, and to serve, not the desire to kill, that had motivated his actions:

> Those who dismiss you merely as a helmeted beast do not understand at all. They do not understand that what you miss when the war has ended is love, for this was the only place in which you were able to truly love your fellow man.[9]

From 1921 to 1924, Montherlant was secretary of the fund to construct the Ossuary of Douaumont in memory of the war dead. He published many articles in the Paris newspapers to raise money for this monument, and these articles form a major part of his *Chant funèbre pour les morts de Verdun* (1924), dedicated to the memory of his comrades.

> Brother by choice that is stronger than blood
> What had you done to be punished?
>
> .   .   .   .
>
> I remain to judge one day
> what happiness could be worth your dying.[10]

Montherlant confessed later that he would not again devote to a burial place all the time and effort he had spent on Douaumont, particularly when he thought of the millions collected for such monuments that could have been used to aid the living.

Because he was certain of the imminence of a new war, Montherlant published the *Chant funèbre pour les morts de Verdun* in 1932, together with all his other unpublished notes on the war, under the title *Mors et Vita*. In these pages, he sought to remind his countrymen of the horrors of war and exhorted them to avoid their repetition. He described what he called the moral armaments forged in the furnace of war, calling for a peace that would present equal opportunities for the display of courage and self-sacrifice.

Montherlant turned to sports after the war in an attempt to recapture the violent activity and virile comradeship of the war years. He explained that sports were war from which the horror had been removed, but where the philosophy remained the same. It was sports that helped to bridge the gap between the "great physical lyricism of war and the bureaucracy of peace." [11] In sports, as in war, there are victories that can be verified by objective appraisal, since man is pitted against man and not against ideas.

> Calm and ordered violence, courage, simplicity, salubrity, something virginal and unpolished, primitive, which does not attempt to analyse itself; that is what I loved in war,

yes, loved, despite all the distress and horror, and that is
what I found again here, that is what these three days a
week give me, the only ones to my measure in a life that is
too small for me.[12]

In 1924, Montherlant published the two volumes of
Les Olympiques, Le Paradis à l'ombre des épées and *Les
Onze devant la porte dorée*, a series of stories, poems,
essays, and a short one-act play, dedicated to soccer and
track. Sports represented for Montherlant an exclusive
"order" which continued the orders of school and war.
The concept of a select group of human beings, bound
together by a common interest and obeying a fixed set of
rules, is to be found throughout Montherlant's work,
particularly his plays. He described the great influence
exerted upon him by such groups in an interview tele-
vised on the B.B.C. in July, 1962:

> My youth, let us say until I was twenty-nine years old, was
> marked above all by communities of men and boys, since
> it is among them that it was spent; the collège, then the
> bullfighting circles, then the war, then the athletic stad-
> ium, then the bullfight again. I made of these milieux—
> two of which, by their very nature, harbored tragedy—a
> place of heroic life. I do not say only "dangerous," I say
> "heroic." During all that period of my life, the world of
> men and boys was linked for me to generosity, to pathos
> and to the best part of myself.[13]

In *Les Olympiques*, Montherlant maintained that
there is no youth on which a mature man can look back
with greater satisfaction than one spent in the sports
arenas. Sports contribute to the formation of both the
body and the character. Although they are neither a
religion nor a system of ethics, they teach a faith more
important than any other, faith in oneself. Sports place
the athlete in contact with reality, since they give him an
understanding of his capabilities and limitations. They
teach him to distinguish between what is important and

what is not, and, at the same time, "to hold tightly to everything while assigning each thing to its proper place." [14] In this way do sports place man in harmony with nature, leading him to seek a synthesis by the process of alternation, a principle of nature which Montherlant was to make the basic principle of his life:

> Like nature, I refuse to choose. I want to delve more deeply into that universal law of rhythm and this divine play of compensations. . . . Happiness, suffering, candor, filth, wisdom, folly, everything belongs to me and I want to have everything, for everything satisfies me only partially. And may I live all lives, all the diversity and contradictions of the world, with intensity and detachment; and let that come to pass, since I will it so. Be able to do everything to experience everything, experience everything to know everything, know everything to understand everything, understand everything to express everything: what a reward the day on which we see ourselves as a mirror of creation and conceive of God in man's image.[15]

His constant desire for new experiences led Montherlant to the bullring in an attempt to recapture there the "hours of poetry" [16] he had lived in the sports stadium. He fought bulls on stock breeding ranches in Spain in 1923, and again in 1925, when he was severely wounded by a bull. In the same year, he wrote the novel *Les Bestiaires*.

The hero of this autobiographical novel, Alban de Bricoule, younger by a few years than the Alban of *Le Songe*, experiences the same emotions on his way to Spain as those felt by the older Alban on his way to the front: "The same excitement, the same desire for great, or at least remarkable things, the same love mixed with a vague apprehension." [17] Alban is drawn to bullfighting by forces greater than himself. He feels that to realize himself, he must kill.

On arriving in Spain, Alban is initiated into the mysteries of the cult of bullfighting, which Montherlant presents as a religious sacrifice inherited from the pagan cult of Mithra, the Sun God. When he was an adolescent, Mithra first struggled with the Sun, then entered into a marvelous friendship with it. With the aid of his dog, Mithra pursued the sacred Bull, conquered it and carried it off into his cave, where he received an order from the Sun to kill it. He suffered, for he loved this wild beast, but killed it despite his love. The sacrifice of the bull created all the goods of the earth. From his blood flowed wine, from his marrow wheat and all vegetation, and from his sperm all animals useful to mankind.[18]

Combined with the mystical aspects, the novel contains realistic and detailed descriptions of both the bullfight and its milieu. The Duke de la Cuesta, a nobleman who raises bulls, befriends Alban and permits him to practice with the bulls on his ranch. The duke's daughter, playing the coquette, promises her favors to Alban in return for his fighting a dangerous bull, which she knows he fears. Alban fights the bull, but punishes Soledad's arrogance and cruelty by spurning her favors afterward. The bullfight serves to affirm the power, virility, and supremacy of man:

It appeared to all that in the center of the arena a sovereign power was at work, which alone was capable of this detachment verging upon disdain: the sovereignty of man was evident to all. It was no longer a combat, it was a religious incantation raised by those pure gestures which were more beautiful than those of love, gestures which not only subdued the animal, but also caused tears to come to the eyes of the vulgar spectators. And he who performed them, raised above the earth like a mystic, lifted by an extraordinary corporeal and spiritual happiness, felt that he was living one of those moments in which we have accomplished something conceived within ourselves and which we call God.[19]

Alban's victory over the bull is symbolic of his power to direct his own destiny. Not only *Les Bestiaires*, but all the works of Montherlant's youth affirm the power and wonder of life. All of them glorify force and express an unquenchable thirst for all pleasures. During these early years, Montherlant sought every opportunity possible to live intensely and gloriously and then fix those moments permanently in his work. His affirmation of life is as basic a reaction of youth as is the despair of the "men of sorrow," who appear in his later works, a reaction of old age:

> The pleasure we give to others and to ourselves has attained its goal, whatever may happen afterward, and thus, only a single hour of true pleasure refutes the concept of the vanity of life. All the more reason for us to fill sixty years with beautiful hours. . . . Then nothingness. Very well, too bad about the void. Do students spoil their vacations with thoughts about going back to school in October? [20]

2

The Hunted Traveler

"The year 1924, in which I published *Les Olympiques* and *Le Chant funèbre pour les morts de Verdun*, brought me fame and took away my taste for it," wrote Montherlant in 1935 in the preface to *Service Inutile.*[1] No longer interested in seeking literary acclaim, Montherlant felt free to leave France after the death of his grandmother in 1925. He did this in an effort to break all ties and to lead what he termed a life of enchantment. His only concern was to deny himself nothing and, by throwing off all obligations, to devote himself solely to realizing his desires. His travels, which were to last for more than seven years, took him to Italy, Spain, and North Africa. The literary result of these travels was the trilogy *Les Voyageurs traqués* (*The Hunted Travelers*). The volumes which make up this trilogy, *Aux Fontaines du désir*, *La Petite Infante de Castille*, *Un Voyageur solitaire est un diable* are, in the words of the author, the diary of the crisis in the life of the thirty-year-old man who stops to take stock of his life "midway between the crisis of adolescence and the one of old age."[2]

In an effort to justify his life of self-indulgence, Montherlant systematized his theory of alternation in an essay of *Aux Fontaines du désir* entitled "Syncrétisme et Alternance." This doctrine, which was first mentioned in

Les Olympiques, arises from a belief in a well-ordered universe. Since everything in nature has its proper place and everything is justified, one must taste of every human experience in order to find happiness. Because simultaneous realization is impossible, it is necessary to alternate within oneself the Angel and the Beast, corporeal, carnal life and moral, intellectual life; for it is essential for a human being to realize that all experiences have their place in the order of things. Whether man wishes to or not, nature, which is constantly in movement, will force him to it. Thus, he should stop denying this essential rhythm of life, recognize it, and abandon himself to it. In this way, he will be able to enjoy, in turn, the variety of human aspirations, all of which emanate from a single source of energy.[3]

Pursuing Montherlant in his new life was what Baudelaire termed man's worst enemy, boredom. He attempted to exorcise the specter of satiety that was haunting him by the refusal of proferred pleasure. In *Aux Fontaines du désir,* he described the joy of renunciation:

> Everything was ready for the great enchantment; . . . The setting, the people: with one word, I would have had everything. I did not say the word. The voluptuousness I experienced was one thousand times greater than what I would have felt had I gone through with it.[4]

Whatever man may obtain cannot compensate for all that eludes him. His desires can never be fully satisfied. After a few years, Montherlant realized that the life he was leading made him no happier than his former existence, and he painted his progressive disillusionment in his notes on *Les Voyageurs traqués:*

> I have reached the flaming ramparts of the world. . . . Nature has said to me . . . : "Think of something new to please you." I no longer can. Things are always the same. . . . I have had too much too often, and too often not

enough. . . . One by one I have seen my reasons for acting submerged, each one in turn, in that rising tide of indifference. . . . The only thing that has remained, together with an inexhaustible love for physical pleasure . . . is the will to write.[5]

The crisis of this period was rendered more acute by the author's ill health. At the end of 1925, he had been gored by a bull, a wound that had never completely healed. During his travels in North Africa, in 1926, he contracted typhoid fever, then pneumonia, and spent four months of that year in nursing homes, suffering at the same time from the delayed effects of his war wounds. "I leave the reader to imagine what it was like to be fifty per cent incapacitated," wrote Montherlant, "for a man who had never had to worry about his body and who had found in the superabundance of energy of this body one of the greatest joys of his youth." [6]

For no apparent reason, the crisis through which he passed began to ease in 1928, and serenity returned in 1929. Life was again as splendid as it had been. Montherlant's renewed happiness resulted in part from his having resolved to his satisfaction the problem of achieving a balance between the art and life of the artist, and the problem of the relationship and exchanges between the two. He stated that during his years of crisis, he had constantly sacrificed his creative ambition to his desires and had been incapable of doing anything other than transcribe his sensations and moods. He had written only the "burning, disjointed pages of a personal diary." [7] Although he regretted the creative void during this period, Montherlant also disapproved of writers who were prepared to remain on the sidelines of life as observers of religion, of war, and of love. He reproached such artists for having failed to realize that the "first duties of the superior man are duties towards himself, duties the common man cannot even imagine." [8]

The conflicting demands made upon the artist are described by Montherlant in great detail in the novel, *L'Histoire d'amour de "La Rose de Sable."* Guiscart, one of the protagonists, is a painter, but could equally well be a writer. He is a libertine who appears much later on in Montherlant's work in the guise of Don Juan. For this man, life is reduced to physical pleasure and he is torn by the effort to satisfy his all-consuming passions and still have time left for creative activity.

Whenever he tried to work, Guiscart was obsessed by all that was escaping him. When he was in his room or his studio, it was rare for a whole hour to go by without his being aroused by a violent impulse which made him go to his window and there, watching the first woman pass by, exclaim passionately to himself: "She, too, is a small portion of happiness being denied me." [9] Although he knew that he would have to pay for this wild life, Guiscart optimistically decided that when he had reached the age when "nights of love are performances rather than pleasures," he would finally, without remorse, devote himself wholly to his work, and seek those honors that are ridiculous for a virile man, but which "sweeten an old age in which, all other passions having been extinguished, there remains alive within us only vanity." [10]

According to Montherlant, there is a certain grandeur in the way Guiscart put off, until a period when his senses failed him, the cultivation of his mind, his soul, and his creative power. To make such a wager with fate, he stated, one must be very sure of the ability of one's nature to keep intact faculties left dormant for so long.

His experiences in North Africa had convinced Montherlant that Guiscart's mode of living was unsatisfactory for him. Neither was he willing to devote his entire life to his work and prepare for himself an old age filled with regret. In an essay of 1937 entitled *L'Art et la Vie,*

Montherlant described the way in which he had resolved this problem, perhaps the most difficult one facing any artist. Recognizing that life is but a matter of hours, he decided to divide his life into two parts only, his work and his pleasure, and to eliminate any wasted time devoted to ego gratification, social ambition, or similar useless pursuits.

A new period of calm and creativity now opened for Montherlant. Far from decrying the time required for his work, he found that it was his work that saved him from the troubles and vexations of the outer world. His literary production during the remaining years preceding World War II falls into two groups: the essays in which he preaches a code of morality to his contemporaries; and the novels which, unlike his earlier lyric constructions, reflect the author's search for objectivity.

3

The Novelist

In 1930, Montherlant wrote a long novel, *La Rose de Sable*, attacking the abuses of French colonialism in North Africa. He decided not to publish the work since he felt that it would be detrimental to French interests. He realized later that the reasons for withholding publication did not apply to the love story, which only touched upon political problems indirectly, and published this part of the novel in 1954 under the title, *L'Histoire d'amour de la "Rose de Sable."* The complete novel was not published until 1968.

The novel deals with the experiences of a young French career officer in North Africa during the early nineteen-thirties. Lucien Auligny, the protagonist, can aspire to a rank no higher than that of major while stationed in France. His ambitious mother arranges to have him transferred from a French provincial garrison to a small outpost in Morocco where advancement is more rapid. There he finds only boredom and stagnation and nothing to divert him from an awareness of his complete uselessness. To relieve his boredom, Auligny arranges to take a fifteen-year-old Arab girl as his mistress. Although their relationship is one of conqueror and conquered, and although he is paying for her favors, Auligny falls in love with Ram. In her attitude towards him, she is like the sand flowers which give their name to the title of the book. These are small masses of sand, petrified into forms ressembling rose petals, all floral grace on the surface, but underneath cold and inert like stones.

Auligny's vision of the Arab world now becomes colored by his feelings for Ram.

> Behind what he loved, he reached out to a world that became alive at his touch. All those movements of fellow feeling he had had for the natives since his arrival in Birbatine required a powerful, intimate emotion like love to tie them together, give them unity and then inundate them with its sap to make them germinate suddenly as if by a miracle. Civilizations, doctrines, landscapes are the palaces of sleeping beauties, inanimate and inert until awakened by a kiss. Yesterday the physical or spiritual domain where we did not love was covered for us by a sea of indifference. And suddenly it exists, it matters intensely to us. We cultivate it, we delve deeply into it, we make it ours. And no one suspects the passions that gave rise to the action that today has become disinterested. And this is all to the good, since people would distrust an adventure of the mind or the conscience that started out as an affair of the heart.[1]

Because of his feelings, he is no longer capable of performing the duties required of a French colonial officer. When his troops leave for an engagement against the Arabs, he refuses to lead them. His reluctance is misunderstood, both by Ram who considers it an act of weakness, and by the French who attribute it to cowardice. Like most men, Auligny prefers to be considered a coward rather than express the difficult truth that his refusal is dictated by his conscience. Even more praiseworthy than his refusal, in Montherlant's opinion, is his knowledge of the uselessness of his sacrifice. It is this recognition that redeems Auligny's mediocre past and makes him a member of the spiritual family of Alban de

Bricoule. Ironically, Auligny is killed by the Arabs he has refused to fight in the course of a native uprising in Fez.

In 1934, the French Academy awarded the "Grand Prix de Littérature" to *Les Célibataires*. This novel, a realistic portrayal of two ruined noblemen who have been unable to adjust to modern society, opens in the manner of the traditional novel with a minute description of setting and clothing.

> At about seven o'clock on this cold winter's evening in February, 1924, a man who appeared to be well on into his sixties, with an unkempt beard of a dirty grey color, stood on one foot in front of a shop on the rue de la Glacière, not far from the boulevard Arago, reading a newspaper by the light of the store window using a large, square stamp collector's magnifying glass. He was dressed in a worn black cloak which reached to his knees and had on his head a dark cap in the style of hats sold around 1885; with a chin strap and two flaps which were turned up on both sides. If anyone had examined him closely, he would have noticed that each detail of his outfit was like that of no one else. His cap had been out of style for thirty years; his cloak was held at the collar by two diaper pins hooked on to each other to form a small chain; the collar attached to his starched white shirt was frayed like lace, revealing the fabric underneath, and his tie was less a tie than a string vaguely covered here and there with a black worn fabric; his baggy trousers were a good fifteen centimeters below what the tailors call the crotch; the lace of one of his enormous boots was a piece of string that someone had tried to paint black with ink.[2]

This introduction to Léon de Coantré prepares the reader for his equally unusual behavior. Léon and his uncle, Elie de Coëtquidan, are two eccentric bachelors who have been living together for years in a town house in Paris.[3] During her lifetime, Léon's mother, the sister of Elie, cared for the two men, neither of whom had ever worked. Upon her death, they are forced to sell their house and, after paying all the debts she incurred to support them, are left virtually penniless. Both seek the aid of Elie's brother, Octave de Coëtquidan, who has made his peace with the twentieth century and achieved financial success. He prides himself on being a "self made man," although he owes his good fortune to the loyalty of an old school friend, who has rewarded his mediocrity with an important position in his bank.

Octave agrees to support Elie when the latter threatens marriage to a Jewish woman who he pretends is his mistress. This kindness exhausts Octave's munificence and he is unwilling to offer similar aid to Léon. Instead, he permits his nephew to occupy the empty gamekeeper's lodge on his country estate. Because of his poverty and his nobility, Léon finds himself surrounded by scorn and hatred, "for all a mystery, and, therefore, a provocation. Irreparably alone." [4]

In his exile, Léon falls ill and visits the country doctor, whose interest in his patients is subordinated to his passion for himself and his hobbies. His disinterest becomes even more pronounced when he discovers that Léon is dependent upon Octave's charity. When Léon pays a return visit to the doctor's office, he is kept waiting for more than an hour. He has reached a state of moral and physical lassitude and for the first time feels affronted at treatment he has accepted without question throughout his life. Having reached the limits of what he can endure, he decides to break with the one man in the world who can save his life, and stalks out of the doctor's office, exclaiming haughtily that he is not the sort of man who will wait for a country doctor. This suicidal act causes a complete change in Léon's opinion of himself. By asserting himself, he has discovered "the formula which permitted him to escape his unhappiness: this formula was pride. . . . And all his misery moved automatically from a sordid to an elevated plane where it ceased to hurt him." [5]

Léon returns to the gamekeeper's lodge to agonize in solitude. His suffering and defeat separate him from the protagonists of Montherlant's early works and bring him close to the heroes of the later plays. His last words are a desperate cry to his former housekeeper, whom he imagines to be in the room, to remain with him because he does not want to die alone. But Léon, like all men, is irrevocably alone and he dies, bound to the earth, to the humming noise overhead of the wild geese who are following the invisible migratory route away from the cold of the north to the warmth and light of the south, "hurrying as if they knew well that one can die for having wasted one moment of happiness." [6]

After Léon's death, his uncle and all those who had refused to help him in his need seek to justify their lack of compassion and charity. They malign the dead man in an effort to prove that he had not merited their kindness. Among the vices unjustly imputed to him is alcoholism. When Octave asks Elie about Léon's drinking, Elie answers that he did not notice anything at the table, but that Léon was free to do as he pleased in his room. The author salutes Elie for this reply because it contains an element of truth, thus proving the author's contention: "It is a great error to place unlimited confidence in men's wickedness: it is rare for them to do us all the harm of which they are capable." [7] Were the entire novel to disappear, Montherlant has written, this maxim would be all he would want to save.

The first two volumes of Montherlant's long novel, Les Jeunes Filles—Les Jeunes Filles and Pitié pour les femmes—followed Les Célibataires by two years. The remaining volumes of this tetralogy—Le Démon du Bien and Les Lépreuses—were published in 1937 and 1939. The inspiration for this work was provided by Montherlant's experiences on the threshold of matrimony. In the preface to *Service Inutile*, Montherlant explained that he had originally accepted the idea of marrying for the sake of social conventions, but then decided to renounce the idea of marriage which began to fill him with horror.

Like Montherlant, Pierre Costals, the hero of *Les Jeunes Filles*, is a writer who is determined to avoid the snare of marriage. The author employs in this diffuse work every modern device of narrative form from newspaper marriage columns to letters, from first person to third person narrative. The thread tying the volumes together is the relationship between Pierre Costals and Andrée Hacquebaut, a provincial, intellectual spinster, and Solange Dandillot, a beautiful and rather stupid young girl. Andrée and Solange represent the soul-body dichotomy symbolized by Dominique and Douce in *Le Songe*.

Andrée, who is isolated because of her intellectual superiority, can find no one other than Costals to her measure. Dissatisfied and unfulfilled, she offers herself to him unconditionally throughout the four volumes, but is always rebuffed by him. He is unable to offer her anything but friendship, but this is not sufficient for "there is only one way to love women, and that is carnally. There is only one way to make them happy, that is to take them in your arms." [8]

Andrée's love disconcerts and annoys Costals. He attributes his repugnance to being loved by her, or by any other woman, to pride, humility, dignity, and a desire for freedom. By pride, he means the male desire to maintain the upper hand and to remain alone even in the act of love. The humility is that of the lucid man who looks at himself objectively and finds himself ridiculous as an object of adoration. His dignity will not allow him to accept the passive role forced upon the beloved, and his desire to remain free will not permit him to be impris-

oned by love. Although he may lose some of his liberty
when it is he who loves, at least this action is controlled
by him, and the pleasure he derives from loving partially
compensates for the loss of liberty. For Costals, love
between man and woman is limited to physical desire.

Sensuality plays a dominant role in all of Montherlant's work. In *Mors et Vita*, the author wrote: "Physical
pleasure is what I have always leaned on in times of
turmoil, as I might rest my hand on a pile of papers in a
rising wind. Let everything else fly away." [9] Elsewhere,
he sings a paean to the joys of physical love, which alone
remain when all else crumbles away:

> If there had been nothing else in my life other than the
> pleasure I received, it would be enough to justify my life,
> which is justified also by the pleasure it has dispensed. It is
> by the giving of pleasure that ordinary humanity redeems
> its stupidity and baseness. What other reason for existing
> have thousands of human beings other than the fact that
> they are, or once were, desirable? [10]

Such overpowering physical desire gives rise to an extremely ambivalent attitude toward women. They are
inferior creatures, but are, at the same time, necessary.
The subjugation of one race by another, symbolized by
the Auligny-Ram relationship, is but a reflection of the
male-female relationship between conqueror and conquered. In describing the first embraces of Costals and
Solange in the Bois de Boulogne, the author compares
his domination of her to the absolute mastery of the bull
by the matador.

Solange Dandillot, the beautiful young woman whom
he makes his mistress, but avoids making his wife, is the
perfect playmate, her beautiful exterior covering a men-
tal vacuum. Her simplicity and passivity, her lack of
ideas, make her all the more desirable to Costals, whose
creator once wrote in his notebooks that he had only to

hear that a girl received a zero in an examination to
make him want to marry her. Solange has absorbed the
conventional social idea that marriage, any sort of marriage, is the only acceptable destiny for a woman, and
will agree to anything in order to become Costals' bride.
This supposedly honorable, Catholic young lady will
agree to fraud, divorce, and even abortion, should the
need arise.

Costals deplores the fact that although woman is
made for one man, man is made for life and for all
women. Man can feel only desire for a woman, which
bores her, and woman can feel only tenderness for man,
which bores him. Their desires, aspirations, views on life
could not be more divergent, yet their destinies are
joined by the sexual act.

> This is the hybrid couple from which stems most of the
> ills of mankind, without either the male or female being
> guilty, but only nature which joined them without suiting
> them to each other.[11]

Marriage is unsuitable for all men, but particularly for
the superior man, the man of genius, since it prevents
him from realizing himself fully. A writer must be able
to move freely from his life to his work at will. Unlike
Guiscart, Costals is unprepared to sacrifice his work to
physical pleasure, each must have its place. He must
rid himself of Solange who has begun to intrude upon
his work. It is only after sending her away that he is
again able to create, and he plunges into his work as he
does into the act of love. Montherlant has maintained
that for the artist the act of creation provides physiologi-
cal relief of the same nature as the act of love. Alone,
Costals leans over the white page, goes back into his
work and regains his integrity. He writes for seventy days
and, on the morning of the "seventy-first day of his
creation," [12] he has had enough and returns to Paris.

To escape again from Solange, he flees from Paris to Morocco to his native mistress and knowingly exposes himself to her leprosy. The disease, for Montherlant, is symbolic of the moral leprosy afflicting Western man, and its symptoms are the refusal to face reality, useless suffering, desire for approbation, gregariousness, and sentimentality. Woman, the source of this infection, is unsatisfactory as a mate, but even more so as a mother of sons. For this reason, Costals has deliberately had a son with a married woman, chosen by him for this purpose, who has renounced all claim to the boy. He is raising the boy secretly at Cannes, away from the contamination of a mother. His housekeeper, who provides all the advantages of maternal love with none of its drawbacks, does not interfere with his efforts to make the boy adopt his moral values. The boy's response to his father's teachings proves him worthy of Costals' love. According to Montherlant, such love between father and son should be placed at the top of the hierarchy of love. Unfortunately, it is extremely rare. The father is generally too busy and too dull-witted to deal with his son in any but a distracted, blundering manner. Boys are only truly loved by born educators or by certain pederasts of the better type.

Thus, in Montherlant's opinion, it is in the love of the mother for the daughter that we find the most perfect form of the love of one human being for another. Solange's mother is vulgar, ignorant, and ridiculous, but she is redeemed by her love for her daughter. After Solange has been abandoned by Costals, Mrs. Dandillot is awakened at night by her concern for her daughter and goes to her room. She kisses her child,

> for her the dearest thing in the world, and this was the same person who made Costals yawn with boredom; the same person whom thousands of men and women passed or jostled indifferently in the street; the same person who would have driven other men mad with desire, without

loving her soul: everything and nothing, powerful and defenseless.[13]

Montherlant describes with great eloquence Mrs. Dandillot's love as she watches her daughter sleep: "How vast is the night over the world and how silent is the earth when one watches one's beloved sleep." [14] Mrs. Dandillot has found the same peace in Solange as Costals did when he returned to his son from his wanderings. For this brief moment, she has achieved the stature of Costals.

Maternal love, disabused paternity, sensuality, the duties of the superior individual towards himself, the problems of education, the grandeur of the superior individual, and the mediocrity of the remainder of humanity are the themes, only more powerfully orchestrated, to be found later on in Montherlant's plays. The one element absent from *Les Jeunes Filles*, with its affirmation of the joys and rewards of creativity and sensuality, is the pessimism and nihilism which constitute the most dominant element of Montherlant's subsequent works. Unlike the later heroes, who are condemned to defeat, Costals emerges victorious from his battle with "Hamour" to confront life on his own terms.

4

A Code of Ethics

In *Les Jeunes Filles*, Montherlant had insisted upon the right of the artist to be free from any demands made upon him by society. He subsequently qualified this to apply only in normal times. In troubled periods, such as in the decade preceding the Second World War, Montherlant stated, the writer's obligations to society took precedence over his right to divorce himself from political involvement. Although he has described the years from 1930 to 1938 as among the happiest in his life, he could not permit his personal happiness to blind him to the world about him. The increasingly volatile political situation after 1935 caused Montherlant grave concern as he saw his apprehensions being realized. The recovery of the Saar, Hitler's repudiation of all treaty limitations on armaments, the reestablishment of universal military service with a standing army of 550,000 men, and the reoccupation of the Rhineland were convincing proof of the approach of the new war with Germany which Montherlant had predicted since the end of the First World War, and for which he had exhorted his countrymen to prepare themselves.

To the threat of war with Germany was added the menace of civil war within France. Before 1936, France had been run as if still in the nineteenth century with her economy controlled by about two hundred wealthy families. In the elections of May 1936, the previously divided Popular Front parties of the left combined to win nearly twice as many seats as the right. The political dominance of the left created a new atmosphere and throughout France workers struck simultaneously, demanding a shorter work week and pay increases. Their demands were granted, preserving France from the riots that might have erupted into civil war. Montherlant, whose sympathies were with the exploited, stated that he would support the workers were there a revolution.[1]

It was the political and moral climate of this era that inspired three volumes of essays in which Montherlant set forth his esthetic and philosophic ideas and proposed a code of behavior for his contemporaries. *Service Inutile* (1935), the first of these volumes, contains the "Letter from a Father to his Son," in which Montherlant describes the moral qualities required to combat what he called the "shopgirl's morality" infecting the French people.

> The virtues you must cultivate above all are moral courage, good citizenship, pride, rectitude, scorn, disinterestedness, politeness, gratitude, and, in a general sense, all that is implied by the word nobility.[2]

The manner in which Montherlant qualified these virtues, in the same letter, served to set him aside from the humanist tradition of Montaigne and Voltaire.

> Many acts that general morality considers innocent condemn a man without recourse. But falsehood, murder, theft, the pillage of war, do not necessarily condemn a man. He may commit them and still retain the attributes of superiority. The life of many men is not worth more than the life of a fish. Theft often has an excuse. Falsehood often does less harm than truth.[3]

According to Montherlant, all that is essential is loftiness of ideals and pride. No weakness such as mercy or charity must be permitted to corrode the metal of a morality more suitable for a warlord than for an ordinary citizen. In all of Montherlant's works, particularly his later plays, we find repeated the idea that every action, however heinous, is acceptable, provided it is performed with nobility, indifference, and pride. In accordance with this code of ethics, only mediocrity is a sin.

Good citizenship, for Montherlant, was synonymous with the patriotic desire to serve one's country both in times of war and of peace. But how was one to serve a country that refused to face facts and prepare for a war it knew to be certain, hoping that it would disappear if ignored? What could be done for a country in which everyone was so engrossed in his own trivial interests and pleasures that he closed his eyes and ears to the dangers until the first bombs began to fall? Knowing that his counsel will be unheeded, the superior individual must continue to speak out in an effort to serve. His service becomes more beautiful as it becomes more meaningless.

The concept of "useless service," which was first expressed by Alban in *Le Songe*, plays a major role in Montherlant's philosophy and dominates the works of his maturity. It lends its name to the series of essays, *Service Inutile*, in which Montherlant's doubt about the efficacy of all action has become radical, nothing has meaning and nothing is worthwhile. Nevertheless, one must act and even serve a cause out of respect for oneself, knowing that it is useless. One must imitate the "soldier-monk" whose passions lead him into combat while his intelligence affirms the vanity of all action. Only in this way may one reconcile the idealism which requires service and the realism which states that such service is useless. "*Aedificabo et destruam*, I will build and then I will destroy what I have built. An epigraph for this book. An epigraph for my life." [4]

The thread which tied together all of the essays of

Service Inutile was Montherlant's desire to serve his countrymen. The essays of *L'Equinoxe de septembre* (1938) were similarly motivated, despite the author's realization at this time of the uselessness of such effort. For twenty years he had been futilely admonishing his countrymen to become strong and to acquire a taste for force so that they would not have to go through another holocaust. To describe his persistence, despite apathy and hostility, Montherlant compared the moralist's message to crops in the field: "They enjoy growing, they take pleasure from the sun and the insects that rest upon them. They are not sad if they are not harvested." ⁵

A vignette, entitled "March 7, 1936," serves as a prologue to *L'Equinoxe de septembre*. It describes a soldier's visit to his father during a short leave. The father, like the rest of the French, had wanted only to be left to himself to spend his remaining years in peace. He had broken all holds the world had upon him, except one, his son. And it is this relationship alone that has given the world a terrible power over him, since it threatens him through what he loves. It is this son who ties him to the world and makes manifest the duties he owes his country, which he has previously ignored. Here again Montherlant affirms his belief in the primacy of man. To Rousseau's cry that without men all would be well, Montherlant replies that without men there would be nothing.

In the essay entitled, "France and the Shopgirl's Morality," the author attempted to explain the shameful attitude of the French people and the French government as they sacrificed Czeckoslovakia at Munich on the day of the September equinox of 1938. Montherlant's disgust with what he considered to be the weakness and mediocrity of the French, caused him to distort the facts and lay the blame for the German victory at the feet of France, for, if she had been strong, there would have been no blond aggression. He compared the French to the Athenians under the yoke of the tyrant Pisistratus and quoted the words of the wise Solon to his countrymen who had not heeded his advice:

> If your meanness has brought you grief, do not blame the Gods for it. It is you, yourselves, who have made these men strong by strengthening them. And that is why you are now undergoing wretched servitude.[6]

Having spoken, he returned to his house, took his arms (for he was an armed wise man) and left them in the street in front of his door. Then, going back into his house, he devoted himself henceforth to writing his poetry. Had Montherlant, himself, done the same at this time, he would have avoided writing *Le Solstice de juin* (1941), a work that brought him condemnation after the war and was one of the principal reasons for his alienation from the postwar generation.

In September 1938, Montherlant was mobilized. On the way to the Maginot Line, he realized that he no longer felt the great fraternal sentiments for his fellow soldiers that he had felt in the first war. Discharged because of poor health, he returned to the front in 1940 as war correspondent for the left-wing newspaper *Marianne*. After the armistice, Montherlant remained in the Midi for a short while and then returned to Paris. His experiences at the front inspired a work, *Le Rêve des guerriers*, which Montherlant destroyed because he felt that it was too cruel an indictment of his countrymen to publish in their defeat. A few selected pages from this work, together with other writings of the period between 1940 and 1944, appeared in *Textes sous une occupation, 1940–1944*, which was published in 1953.

It is difficult to imagine in what way this book could have been more harmful than *Le Solstice de juin*. In the latter work, in addition to a reiteration of his moral precepts, and criticism of French mistakes and lack of aggressiveness, Montherlant exalts the swastika, which he had hailed in *L'Equinoxe de septembre* as the symbol of the masculine principle that would vanquish the feminine, emasculating doctrine of Christianity. The swastika is derived from the four-spoked wheel and from the disk which formerly represented the sun. This solar wheel is also a symbol of alternation, one of the principles guiding Montherlant's life. Since alternation was the principle governing the universe and would, in time, bring another Christian victory, Montherlant counseled wholehearted acceptance of the German victory.

> A double acceptance: acceptance of reality and acceptance of a fair occurrence . . . we were beaten absolutely fairly, and in every respect. Acceptance, then adherence.[7]

Again, in the essay, "The Caterpillars," in the same volume, Montherlant counseled the adoption of the rules of sport in which one does all he can to defeat the adversary, "but once he has shown himself victorious, ally yourself wholeheartedly with him." [8]

Intoxicated by the sheer force of the virile Germans, Montherlant directed his anger not against these "pagans," but against the weak French army in retreat, exhaling the special odor of defeat:

> Each one of those French faces, each so different from the other, passed by with its own expression of despair, as if they had been told in a playful contest to assume expressions of despair. I had the same indifference for these defeated armies as one has for the picador's horse who, when thrown to the ground, becomes entangled in its intestines. The center of interest was elsewhere.[9]

Because of *Le Solstice de juin*, Montherlant was severely criticized after the war. His partisans ignored this work and maintained that his was a crime of omission rather than of commission and that he had the right to remain independent during the occupation of his country. It is as difficult to accept this defense as it is to understand the motivation behind *Le Solstice de juin*. From his earliest works, Montherlant had expressed a great love for his country and had involved himself in efforts to awaken it to the danger with which it was threatened. In 1934, in *Service Inutile*, Montherlant had written that a writer who buries himself in his work when his country is in danger, paves the way for remorse. For, on the day on which the crisis is resolved, he will either reap benefits procured by others or he will suffer because of a yoke that he could have helped to break. By abstaining, Montherlant added, "he betrayed not only his compatriots, but also, in some measure, the work in the name of which he betrayed them." [10] While Montherlant was never accused of active collaboration, his acceptance of the "new order" was a crime in the light of his own principles.

After the war, he was censured by the National Committee of Writers, a Resistance organization. As a formality, a twelve-month retroactive ban on publication was imposed, a ban that was meaningless since he had already published during the period covered by the ban. His actions, however, had cut him off from the mainspring of French life. Montherlant's generation had hailed him principally as a moralist, but the postwar generation turned to writers like André Malraux, Jean-Paul Sartre and Albert Camus, who had been actively engaged in the struggle for freedom. They were indifferent to the counsel of a man who had been unable to accord his own life to his principles. Montherlant had said in *L'Equinoxe de septembre* that France would be saved by those of her sons who possessed the courage "to refuse to play the game, the courage to say no, the courage to be severe, the courage to be unpopular." [11] When these sons finally appeared in the ranks of the Resistance, Montherlant was not there.

After 1941, Montherlant turned to the theater, which offered him a means for withdrawing from the public controversy. This medium permitted him to attain a certain degree of artistic objectivity, infusing life into a wide variety of characters, while, at the same time, still expressing his philosophy through the protagonist of each play who is his personal spokesman. The moralist, who had judged and proposed rules of conduct, became the psychologist, who observed and analysed human behavior objectively, without moral judgment.

5

The "Christian Vein"

The desire to go beyond and surpass oneself, a passion
for purity, the will to transpose life to a higher plane,
and the pursuit of an ideal, carrying with it a feeling of
elevation, are common to all of Montherlant's work.
Although these ideals may be regarded as religious in
essence, the moral values and rules of conduct ex-
pounded by Montherlant are not those of Christian morality.

La Relève du matin, his first work, was hailed upon
publication as a Catholic work because of its sympa-
thetic portrayal of the Catholic *collège.* In a preface
added to a later edition of the book, Montherlant sought
to explain his subsequent ambivalent attitude toward
religion. He maintained that even in *La Relève du matin*
he had expressed doubt about the truth of Catholicism
several times, and that sentences questioning the existence of God had alternated with those affirming belief in
Him. He added that although he had never been a true
Christian, he had always been someone for whom good
and evil existed and who adored what he called the
natural morality existing behind the external trappings
of the Catholic church.

In *Pour une Vierge noire* of 1930, Montherlant repeated that while he does not believe in Christianity as a
revealed religion, he does not reject all of its dogma. As

36

evidence of this conflicting attitude, he has alternated in his work a "Christian vein and a profane vein." [1] However, even in those works which he includes in his Catholic vein, the Catholic religion has served Montherlant as a source of inspiration rather than as a spiritual guide. The fact that he is less interested in the faith itself than in those who have faith is best illustrated in Montherlant's four Catholic plays: *Le Maître de Santiago, La Ville dont le Prince est un enfant, Port-Royal,* and *Le Cardinal d'Espagne.* Although the subject matter is borrowed directly from the history of Catholicism, the characters in these plays possess and are motivated by purely earthly sentiments.

Maurice Barrès, who exerted a considerable influence on the young Montherlant, spoke of "places which draw a soul out of its lethargy, places that are enveloped and bathed in mystery, elected for all eternity as the seat of religious emotion." [2] The Catholic *collège,* which Montherlant depicted in *La Relève du matin,* and, much later, in *La Ville dont le Prince est un enfant* and *Les Garçons* was, for him, such a place.

In *La Ville dont le Prince est un enfant,* two students, Sevrais and Soubrier, are united in an intimate, exclusive friendship. The Abbé de Pradts discovers their liaison, which violates the rules of the school. After denouncing them from the pulpit, he persuades the older boy, Sevrais, to repudiate the emotional side of the relationship. Sevrais exults at the idea of transposing their friendship to a higher plane but, tricked by the Abbé who is also passionately attached to Soubrier, gives his rival the opportunity to expel him. The Abbé's victory is short-lived. The Superior of the institution, who has divined the dangerous passion motivating the Abbé, sends Soubrier away and forbids the Abbé all further relationship with the boy.

Although Montherlant has called this a religious play,

God is mentioned only in the final scene with the entrance of the Superior. Even then, it is not religion, but order that triumphs. Everything is returned to its proper place and discipline is reestablished. Nevertheless, there is still a distinct religious presence in this tragedy of sacrifice and elevation. It has been observed that the very absence of God throughout four-fifths of the play is so oppressive, that it becomes equal to a presence.[3] Montherlant has remarked that there is divine grace in all of the characters in this play because, for him, wherever there is elevation of sentiments there is grace.

In an essay, entitled "Three Days at Montserrat," Montherlant expressed his sympathy for the Jansenist religious sect,[4] which was centered in seventeenth-century France in the convent of Port-Royal.

> I know that if I ever decided to take Catholicism seriously, I would follow the path nearest to its heart. It is a tradition that goes from the Gospel to Port-Royal by way of Saint Paul and Saint Augustine.[5]

Montherlant's interest in the order culminated in the play *Port-Royal*. The plot, which is historical, is based on Chapter II, Book V of Sainte-Beuve's history of the Jansenist movement. It deals with the refusal of the Sisters of Port-Royal, led by Sister Angélique Arnauld, to comply with the wishes of the Church hierarchy that they sign a paper admitting the presence of certain heretical propositions in the writings of Jansen, the spiritual founder of the order. Because of their refusal, the Archbishop Péréfixe denies them the right to participate in the holy sacraments and exiles the twelve most rebellious Sisters from the convent.

In the preface to the play, Montherlant stated that his aim was to show Christianity under one of the guises it has assumed during the course of history. Since he was not concerned with the theological basis of the controversy, he omitted the debate between free-will and pre-destination. Montherlant's preoccupation with personal liberty may be another reason for his having stifled all religious debate in this play. Historically, the Jansenists, by their espousal of the doctrine of predestination, which affirms the inability of the individual to mold his own destiny, were the enemies of liberty. In the conflict presented in Montherlant's play, it is the Jansenists who defend the right of the individual to act according to the dictates of his own conscience. The Church and State, banded together, represent society which fears and perse-cutes the nonconformist.

Despite the absence of all metaphysical elements, there is in this play a certain spiritual interplay of dia-metrically opposed religious sentiments. The persecution produces a loss of faith in Sister Angélique while it strengthens the faith of Sister Françoise, who becomes more courageous as the persecution intensifies.

In *Le Maître de Santiago*, Montherlant depicts an-other historical era of Christianity, that of sixteenth-cen-tury Castille, a period that produced men who, "after the age of fifty, withdrew from the world with their rigid faith, their scorn for external reality, their liking for ruin, their passion for nothingness." [6] El Greco depicted this type of man in his painting of Julian Romero, Com-mander of the Order of Santiago, being presented to God by the "Knight of the Fleurs-de-lys." Montherlant includes this portrait in every edition of his play since, for him, it expresses the splendid affirmation of faith of these men.

Don Alvaro Dabo, the protagonist of *Le Maître de Santiago*, belongs to this family of men. His friend, Don Bernal, asks him to participate in an expedition to Amer-ica to amass the dowry that would permit his daughter, Mariana, to marry Don Bernal's son. Alvaro refuses, both because he condemns the Spanish exploitation of the Indians, and because he will tolerate no interference with his ascetic existence. Don Bernal, knowing that Alvaro will not refuse his sovereign, persuades Mariana to permit a courtier to tell Alvaro that the king wishes a man of his stature in the colonies. Just as Alvaro is about to renounce his principles on the strength of this false request, the stratagem is revealed by Mariana. She then emulates her father by renouncing the world to enter a convent.

In the postface to *Le Maître de Santiago*, Montherlant states that he has not made of Alvaro a model Christian, but rather one who remains on the fringes of Christianity. He adds that Alvaro feels strongly the first tenet of Christianity, which is the renunciation of earthly goods and ties, the *Nada*, but ignores the second, which is the *Todo* or the union with God and all of God's creatures in love. Islamism strongly influenced the Spain of this period and Alvaro's religion, like that of Islam or that of the Old Testament, reveres the infinite distance separating man from God. Consequently, he ignores the tender intimacy with Christ. Alvaro is separated from both God and his fellowman by his supreme ego and, because he is incapable of any sort of communion, lives in a state of illusory saintliness which he equates with passivity: "I am waiting for everything to end." [7] While Alvaro's faith may be incomplete, the atmosphere of the play is essentially religious, stressing the requisites for a truly spiritual life: asceticism, a feeling of exaltation, the desire for solitude, a passion for purity, and a will for perfection. Although Alvaro is devoid of Christian charity, he is imbued with a Christian passion for purity and the desire to transpose life to a higher plane.

In *Le Cardinal d'Espagne*, Church history is again used to provoke a dramatic conflict between the desire for worldly participation and recognition, and the desire for withdrawal. Francisco Ximenez de Cisneros, Archbishop of Toledo, Primate of Spain, Grand Chancellor, Grand Inquisitor, and Regent of Castille, has succeeded in having the future Charles V proclaimed king of Castille, to rule jointly with his mother, Joanna the Mad. The Cardinal who, through cruelty and oppression, has sought to keep Spain mighty for the glory of God, awaits the arrival in Castille of the young king who, he is sure, will have need of his services. When he visits the mad, sequestered queen, Cisneros is tempted by her to renounce the world to enter into the nothingness of which she has become part and which is a step toward God. The queen tells him that he has constantly deceived himself, and that his three flights from power into a monastery were motivated not by religious fervor, but by a desire to be recalled into the world and granted ever greater temporal power.

The Cardinal's great-nephew, Cardona, also tries to provoke him to destroy the work he has accomplished in this world as a step toward God. Although he is profoundly moved, Cisneros cannot renounce power, to which he is inescapably drawn. When the young king sends a message ordering the Cardinal back to his monastery and the silence he supposedly has craved, he dies from the blow to his pride and his worldly aspirations. The struggle within Cisneros is between action and contemplation, religious faith never really intervenes. With faith, Cisneros' struggle would have been directed against his worldly inclinations. Because he is a statesman rather than a man of God, he has no supreme reason for renouncing them:

> I would be ready to run the risk of going to hell, if at that price I could do good for the State. But the designs of God and those of the government of Castille have always been identical. Besides, you may be unaware of the fact that I have a system of silent prayer which permits me to

cancel out my political actions before God as I perform them.[8]

The sensual Catholicism of the Italian Renaissance, so different from the Spanish asceticism, has also inspired Montherlant. In *Malatesta,* he portrays this casual Catholicism practiced by the devout *condottiere* of that time, with both a dagger and a rosary in his pockets, with both mistresses and a confessor close at hand. Sigismond Pandolphe Malatesta, Lord of the feudal city of Rimini, receives a request from the Pope to allow papal troops to occupy Rimini. In exchange, Malatesta would be granted sovereignty over the cities of Spoleto and Foligno. Driven into a fury by this ruse to deprive him of Rimini, Malatesta assigns to Porcellio, a writer in his employ, the mission of killing the Pope. The wily Porcellio persuades Malatesta to attempt the murder himself. The Pope, sensing that Malatesta means him harm, is able to escape assassination. Feigning clemency, he appoints Malatesta *condottiere* of the papal troops in order to confine him to Rome where he can be kept under surveillance. Acceding to the entreaties of Isotta, Malatesta's wife, the Pope permits him to return to Rimini for a few months. It is in Rimini that Malatesta meets his death, murdered by Porcellio, whose resentment of the gratitude he owes Malatesta for once having saved his life, has poisoned his entire existence.

The Renaissance Catholicism depicted in *Malatesta* is impregnated with the culture of Antiquity. All of Malatesta's words and actions reveal an alternation of paganism and Catholicism.

> Good fortune of the Malatesta family . . . be favorable to me! *I* will make you a gift of an entire year without sin: yes, an entire year of virtuous living and great offerings to the poor, and a sincere repentence for my faults, if you permit me to kill the Pope and not be killed while doing it.[9]

Sometimes, for double security, he also entrusts himself to the Holy Virgin. At times he even invokes Divine Providence, but only to give it thanks for his mistress Vanella, blessing it for having permitted his sin. His unconscious, spontaneous mixture of paganism and Catholicism is reflected in the temple he is building in Rimini in which all of the decorations, inscriptions, and symbols are inspired by pagan legends.

Montherlant has described Ferrante, the protagonist of *La Reine morte*, as a type of Christian quite prevalent in the Middle Ages, one whose evil tendencies were never inhibited by his religion, yet who constantly made reference to his faith. Ferrante, king of Portugal, wants his son Pedro to marry the Infanta of Navarre for political reasons. He learns that Inès de Castro, one of the ladies of the court, is secretly married to his son and that she is about to bear him an heir. Ostensibly because this marriage represents a menace to the state, but in reality for much more profound reasons, the king, spurred on by his advisor, Egas Coelho, has her assassinated. Ferrante dies immediately thereafter and Pedro, the new king, crowns his wife posthumously.

God is very much alive for Ferrante and, in all of his moments of trouble, he invokes His name and calls to Him. He is certain that he will achieve salvation. Ferrante is irresistibly drawn to committing what he knows to be a great crime. He cannot withstand the temptation to plunge into the abyss. One of Montherlant's critics has observed that Ferrante is the Christian drawn towards sin by an implacable fatality, by impulses he cannot combat without the help of divine grace. He notes further that this drama, which illustrates the fatality of sin, pushes Jansenism to its most extreme consequences.[10]

Montherlant has never accepted Christian rules of conduct which make a sharp distinction between good and evil. He has substituted for the Christian concept of sin the idea that only mediocrity is a sin. It has been noted that everything in Montherlant's work is directed towards achieving the greatest glory for man and that when man renounces his pleasure, it is only to increase his stature and reaffirm his liberty by a victory over himself.[11] Montherlant also rejects the consoling aspect of the Christian faith which places its trust in a future life in which the just will be rewarded.

Despite all of this, there is a discernible Christian element in Montherlant's work, evidenced by his interest in the human soul, his pursuit of an ideal, and his constant search for a higher form of existence. In one of the poems of *Encore un instant de bonheur*, Montherlant expressed the desire which can never be satisfied on this earth:

> if I had risen to the highest of all spheres,
> I would still feel myself to be a prisoner and would want to climb higher.[12]

Montherlant has been described as an incomplete Christian.[13] Despite the Christian influences in his work, there is much in Christianity that is absent from it. The pride, renunciation, splendor, and severity extolled by Montherlant are also in Christianity, but in Christianity they are fused with the love and charity absent from Montherlant's universe.

6

The Dramatic Hero

Montherlant chose the theater as a means of expression after he had achieved renown as an essayist and novelist. His present reputation rests principally on his plays which, other than *L'Exil* and the dramatic poem *Pasiphaé*,[1] date from the appearance of *La Reine morte* in 1942. In writing for the theater, Montherlant did not divorce himself from the novelist and the essayist, for his plays, like his earlier works, express his philosophical ideas and moral principles. It is in the theater that Montherlant's hero achieves his full stature.

All of the protagonists in Montherlant's plays, despite their differences, belong to the same spiritual family. All struggle to realize what the Infanta of *La Reine morte* called "the great things within themselves." [2] In order to achieve their noble ideals, they strive constantly for personal liberty, for freedom from common duties and obligations. It is for this reason that many of them appear in the guise of exceptional, semilegendary persons who would naturally be exempt from the restrictions and limitations imposed upon ordinary humans.[3] This liberty need not necessarily be that of rulers like Ferrante, Pasiphaé, Cisneros, and Malatesta, but can also be the moral liberation achieved by certain superior members of bourgeois society. Georges Carrion, the protagonist of *Fils de personne*, refuses to conform to the base standards set by

45

contemporary society. He will adhere only to his own moral principles. He attempts to instill these principles into his illegitimate son, Gillou, whom he has met by chance after twelve years of neglect. He becomes interested in the boy he has never known and takes refuge with him and his mother in the south of France after the armistice of June, 1940. During the ensuing months, Georges makes a determined effort to develop the boy's character, but becomes exasperated by Gillou's unshakable mediocrity and finally severs relations with him. Despite Gillou's age, he has already revealed the mediocre adult he will become. He possesses none of the qualities Montherlant found so attractive in adolescence, and which are possessed by the adolescents in La Ville dont le Prince est un enfant. The young Sevrais is the only character in all of Montherlant's plays who is capable of a sincerely disinterested act. The Abbé de Pradts remarks that this is probably the last time in his life that he will have such an unselfish liaison. The boy is capable of spontaneous acts of generosity because he has not yet settled into a fixed pattern of life.

It is because Pedro in La Reine morte has traded the freedom of adolescence for the fetters of manhood, that Ferrante rejects him. He loved his son when he was young, but he has since become a man, that is to say "the caricature of what he once was." [4] He has lost the grace, finesse, and intelligence he possessed at the age of thirteen, the most glorious year of his life. Striking contrast exists between Ferrante's attitude towards Pedro and his reactions to the young pages with whom he surrounds himself. In them, he finds the purity that precedes manhood. Even if they practice deceit and betrayal, as does the page Dino del Moro who betrays Ferrante, these actions are performed with such spontaneity, that even defects and vices, when they are sincere reactions of an unrestrained and intuitive nature, become positive qualities. And all that is natural, spontaneous, and uncorrupted by society is good.

After their adolescence, Montherlant scorns young men, except for a few chosen individuals who retain, even in maturity, the qualities of the adolescent. Malatesta, whose imagination is capable of the dreams and fantasies of youth, is the eternal adolescent. He is driven by his desires and gives way to the inspiration of the moment, committing absurd actions although realizing full well their imprudence. Like nature, he is in a constant state of change. "It is in those whom God loves best that concepts change most often; He expresses in these particularly rich souls several fragments of His truth." [5] Despite the fact that Malatesta is an adulterer, a murderer, that he has attempted unnatural sexual acts with his son and committed innumerable antisocial acts, "infinity is on the side of Malatesta," [6] by virtue of his constant efforts to realize all of his potentialities.

Like Alban in the early novels, all of Montherlant's theatrical heroes are driven by the desire to experience all that life has to offer, free from the restraints of any established moral code. The liberties offered by war represent for Philippe, the protagonist of *L'Exil*, a unique opportunity to attain self-fulfillment. When he learns that his best friend, Sénac, has just enlisted in the army, Philippe decides to join him. He sees war as a suspension of everyday life, permitting those who participate liberties denied to others. At the front, he can lead the richest life possible, participate in the great adventure, and achieve glory. War presents the opportunity, states Philippe, "to live, to suffer, to love, to give of myself, to transform myself in accordance with what is best in me." [7]

Philippe's mother, Geneviève, who has been risking her own life in the ambulance corps, begs him to remain behind in safety. Philippe reluctantly agrees, but tells her that he will be a constant reproach to her, that she will suffer on seeing his unhappiness and that, eventually, it will be she who begs him to leave. Philippe's unsatisfied desire continues to haunt his mind and poison his existence. Deprived of the war, he incurs the scorn of those about him by his affected cynicism. After several months, Geneviève, realizing his humiliation and seeing that she has lost his love, tells him to go. Her decision comes too late. Sénac has been wounded and is returning to Paris. It is now Philippe who refuses to leave. The friends' reunion is a mutual disappointment since Sénac's experiences have alienated him from Philippe. They decide to sever relations. But the victory does not belong to Geneviève, for Philippe enlists immediately thereafter. At the front, he hopes to fashion for himself a soul like that of his friend, one that has been enriched by the experiences and comradeship of war.

Pasiphaé will not recoil before her monstrous desire. Her passion rises up before her like a challenge. She must accomplish her union with the bull to deliver herself of this act, to put an end to the obsession which shuts her off from the universe, so that she may once again be at peace with the world. Montherlant regards her passion as a sign of health. He, too, he stated, has desired "animals, plants, women, close relatives." [8] He believes that men who have limited desires have limited souls.

To satisfy her passion, Pasiphaé must face the blame and condemnation of all, she must challenge the morality and prejudices of society. In the preface to *Pasiphaé*, Montherlant explained that he deliberately discarded the popular interpretation which portrays her as a goddess who augments her divine power by uniting with the bull. He preferred to present her as a mortal queen, deliberately defying all the customs of Crete. She does so with courage, scorning the judgments of mankind which "cover us like worms," [9] and goes forward to her desire without remorse in order to accomplish an act that gnaws at her soul. She will have dared what no one has ever dared and, by so doing, will have raised herself above ordinary mortals to prove herself worthy to be a queen. It is not important that this act will afford her no pleasure, for she will have defied death by realizing her desires.

Montherlant admires the universality of the Renaissance hero who accomplished his destiny by accepting and even emphasizing the contradictions within himself. The Renaissance hero sought the full development of his physical and moral faculties and attempted to merge harmoniously all the contrasts existing within him. Such a hero is Malatesta who, by actions such as his attempted murder of the Pope, provokes his destiny and creates opportunities to escape from the ordinary. His disgrace and virtual imprisonment in Rome are as important as his successes in contributing to his glory, for such vicissitudes of fortune repeat the rhythm of nature. Malatesta is certain of his glory and seeks to perpetuate his name in the verses of his hired poet and in the marble of his temple.

All of Montherlant's protagonists are heroic in their quest for glory, not the glory conferred by others, but the one they find within themselves. This idea has not changed in Montherlant's work since his early statement:

> you are your own goal, and this goal is sufficient and it is glorious. It is yourself whom you respect. It is only before yourself that you stand to be judged. [10]

To their love of inner glory, may be added grandeur of soul and honor, qualities which, according to the critic Pierre-Henri Simon, characterize the hero. The hero, writes Mr. Simon, loves struggle, victory, and power, and is best characterized by his devotion to the realization of noble goals. This concept of heroism is closely allied to that of nobility, since both of them affirm an exceptional origin and moral superiority.[11]

Since heroic theater requires a lofty vocabulary, Montherlant, like Corneille, emphasizes words like "merit," "quality" and "esteem," words he defined previously in his "Letter from a Father to his Son." There is an indefinable essence that sets the superior person apart, a quality that causes him to be disgusted with evil. Montherlant stated in the same essay that, if anything prevented him from having a son, it was precisely the fear that the boy would be lacking in quality. The apprehension he expressed in 1935, and again in *Les Jeunes Filles*, is dramatically realized in *Fils de personne*, where a son's mediocrity makes his father despair of all humanity. Gillou delights only in false values and has an instinctive antipathy to anything worthwhile. He lacks quality which is, "like, in the case of the tuning fork, the pure, fundamental sound emitted by an unblemished, undamaged nature when it comes into contact with the outer world." [12]

Such a "pure note" exists within Persilès, the protagonist of the play *Brocéliande*, who liberates himself from the mediocre, bourgeois life he has led for sixty years when he is informed by a genealogist that he is a remote descendant of Saint Louis. This revelation transforms his life, for it creates within him the desire to prove himself worthy of his noble ancestor. His dreams give him insight into another life where he can live unrestricted by social constraints. He is only able to experience the noble sentiments which should accompany such an exalted position because his basic sentiments were worthwhile. He had needed only the proper stimulus to permit him to rise above his situation in life. When his wife, in her jealousy, reveals to him that there are fifteen thousand people in France with whom he shares his distinction, he kills himself.

Characteristic also of the hero is his boundless egotism, the knowledge of his own worth and superiority. A necessary concomitant of this grandeur is a longing for a higher form of life. It is not sufficient for the exceptional person to live, it is necessary that he live gloriously. He seeks a more exalted life in the midst of others who tend only to facility and compromise. The hero scorns the vulgar and the utilitarian as he detests the weak and sentimental; for all these are manifestations of mediocrity. No matter what the setting of the play may be, all of Montherlant's heroes are disgusted with the pettiness and corruption of those surrounding them. Alvaro, to whom God has given in profusion the "virtue of disgust," condemns the cruelty and dishonesty of the Spanish colonizers in America in their exploitation of the Indians. He is disgusted with their passion for profit and gold. Spain has become for him a source of humiliation and he cries out bitterly:

> There is nothing for me to do at a time when honor is punished,—when generosity is punished,—when charity is punished,—when everything that is great is disparaged and mocked,—where everywhere in the front ranks I see trash,—where everywhere the triumph of the most stupid and the most abject is assured.[13]

Montherlant has called his heroes "masters of scorn." Their scorn is directed against the sin of the mind—stupidity—and against the sin of the soul—baseness.[14] They scorn the mediocre desire for happiness, so beneath their desire for grandeur.

Throughout Montherlant's drama, we find a conflict between the desire for grandeur and the desire for happiness. In his *Carnet* XLII of 1942, Montherlant noted that one of the keys to contemporary French mentality is the desire for well-being, from which stems the vice of living great tragedies in bourgeois fashion.[15] Nowhere is this conflict more clearly illustrated than in Act I, Scene 3 of *La Reine morte*, in which Pedro defends his rights to the happiness of a private citizen against the imperious duties of the throne. Ferrante then reproaches him, declaring that he does not breathe at the same heights as his father. To this, Pedro replies that private life is important, that it, too, carries its responsibilities, and that molding the lives of a woman and child and giving them a happiness that they would never have experienced without you, should take precedence over all else. Besides, having only forty years at the most to live, he wishes to make them as happy as possible. These words, epitomizing mediocrity for Ferrante, arouse him to ask Pedro harshly whether he is a woman to think only of his happiness. Here, he expresses the recurrent theme in Montherlant's work that the mediocre desire for happiness is a feminine trait. In his anger, Ferrante orders Pedro to prison for mediocrity, a crime he considers more serious than any other.

Another commonplace sentiment attacked is naïveté. Ferrante remarks that although he hates vice and crime, he prefers them immeasurably to naïveté, and he feels an irresistible desire to put the trusting Inès in contact with reality, to disabuse her and show her the world as it really is.

Love between man and woman, or between parent and child, is another form of debasement. This does not include physical desire which finds grace in Montherlant's eyes since it is a basic instinct of man's nature. Love is rather that emotional attachment which destroys either the lover or the loved one. Pedro is fit for nothing else once he has been ensnared by his love for Inès. Isotta's protective love for Malatesta is the cause of his undoing, since her nervous premonitions instill in him a moral weakness which makes him easy prey for Porcellio. Ironically, it is also she who calls Porcellio back, leaving him alone with the victim she has inadvertently prepared for him. Even Mariana's love for Don Jacinto does not escape Alvaro's condemnation. Despite the fact that, in marriage, she aspires to a life which would require a great deal of courage, one in which she could be useful to her husband in serious and grave matters, Alvaro still exults in her decision to renounce the world. In this way, she will never have known the infection of man's love.

There is no place for natural love between parents and children, for unless love is based on esteem it is meaningless and second-rate. Ferrante states that blood relationship is without value and that there is only one link, the one with people whom one esteems. Georges, tormented by Gillou's mediocrity, exclaims that he loves his son, that he would like to esteem him as much as he loves him, but cannot do so. He begs him pathetically to act and think in a fashion that would permit his father to be proud of him as a son. He loves Gillou in the only fashion in which most of Montherlant's heroes can love, with the will to modify the object of his love and refashion it to his own measure.

Since it cannot be elevated, mediocrity must be destroyed without mercy. All of Montherlant's heroes are completely lacking in sympathy and mercy, traits which, together with gentleness, are considered marks of mediocrity. Egas Coelho, one of the king's advisors in *La Reine morte*, counsels severity, stating that "to be merciful one only has to give way, but to be firm one must raise oneself." [16] To prove the worth of his ideas, the hero must never reject the course of action he deems necessary, no matter how cruel it may appear. He must sacrifice all that stands in the way of the realization of his ideals.

Montherlant has been obsessed with the idea of sacrifice since his earliest works. This may account for his attraction to the religion of the pagan god Mithra, with its ritual sacrifice of the bull. The sacrifice of the bull, like sacrifice in all religions, is a supernatural ritual by means of which one communicates with the divinity through the intermediary of a victim. The blood of the victim serves as a means of regeneration for the person who performs the sacrifice. Sacrifice is also the law of life, for in nature each thing must disappear in its turn to make room for and nourish the new. It has been stated that each of Montherlant's plays is a series of debates preceding capital executions, the main body of the play representing the ritual leading up to the final sacrifice.[17]

The sacrifice of one's children has been of particular interest to Montherlant, who has observed that Abraham's proposed sacrifice of Isaac exerted a strong influence on his theater. While Abraham was prepared to sacrifice his son to prove his devotion to God, Montherlant's heroes sacrifice their offspring to assure the victory of their own principles. In *Fils de personne*, Georges Carrion sacrifices his son to the principle of human quality. In *Demain il fera jour*, the sequel to this play, which takes place four years later, Georges again sacrifices Gillou, this time to his fear. Georges, who has deteriorated morally, is in Paris with Marie and Gillou. The boy wishes to join the Resistance, but Georges refuses to allow him to do so until he receives an anonymous letter, threatening him with reprisals after the war for having collaborated with the enemy. Georges then gives his permission, hoping that Gillou's patriotic activities will protect him when the war has ended. On his first mission, Gillou is killed.

Sacrifice need not be the immolation of another. Montherlant has expressed his admiration for the Greek philosopher Peregrinos who, having experienced all the diversities of life and finding himself incapable of

inventing anything new which might excite the admiration of the spectators or satisfy his ardent thirst for glory,
invented the mad idea of sacrificing himself on a burning
pyre.[18] This action of Peregrinos, which has always been
misunderstood and ridiculed by posterity, excites only
admiration in Montherlant, who declares that "a man
who kills himself for a moral principle, even supposing
the moral principle to be of questionable value, deserves
to be praised." [19]

The subject of suicide is discussed at great length by
Montherlant in his notebooks of 1958 to 1964, to which
he has given the title *Va jouer avec cette poussière*. Since
earliest times, with certain exceptions, suicide has always
been regarded as a crime committed by those who have
been defeated by life. Montherlant disagrees, for he regards suicide rather as an act of defiance, "the last act by
which a man can show that he dominated life and was
not dominated by it." [20] Suicide has fascinated Montherlant since he first read about it in the pages of *Quo
Vadis*, which described the elegant death of Petronius
who, having opened his veins, made dying a leisurely
procedure accompanied by festivity. In Montherlant's
play, *La Guerre Civile* (1965), there is only one suicide,
but the author notes that he was particularly impressed
by the fact that, historically, all the people of merit who
appear in the play, kill themselves at a later date. The
action of Montherlant's play takes place in the camps of
Caesar and Pompey in the south of Dyrrachium (today
Durazzo, Albania), exactly three weeks before the defeat
of Pompey by Caesar at Pharsala. The protagonist of this
play is Pompey, complex, inconsistent, subject like Malatesta to nervous depressions, one of which will lead to his
later downfall. In his exchanges with his general, Cato
the Younger, it is Cato who speaks for Montherlant and
whose actions epitomize useless service, as he fights for a
cause in which he does not believe and for a leader in

whom he does not believe. The one dramatic incident in this otherwise static play is the suicide on stage of Acilius, a captain in Caesar's army, who has been captured by Pompey's forces. The prisoner is brought before Pompey. In a gesture to prove his power, Pompey grants Acilius his freedom. Rather than owe his life to a man he despises, Acilius seizes a sword and plunges it into his own throat. He crumbles at Pompey's feet. Pompey recoils, then signals for no one to touch Acilius. While they watch him convulsed in agony, Domitius turns his head away in a profound gesture of shame. Those closest to the dying man move away little by little in order to keep their feet out of the blood which continues to spread.

In all of Montherlant's plays, the sacrifice, whether of others or of oneself, is motivated by scorn and disdain, except for *La Ville dont le Prince est un enfant*, which Montherlant has called "a tragedy of sacrifice. . . . The ladder of sacrifices which is built from scene to scene in the third act is presented by certain of my principle characters as a ladder which mounts to God." [21] In this play, all of the principal characters struggle to renounce their passions. After Sevrais and Soubrier have been discovered together by the Abbé de Pradts, in violation of the rules, Sevrais learns that he is to be expelled from the school and that he must no longer see Soubrier. Because of his noble character, he is able to overcome his initial reaction of revolt and sacrifice his deep friendship for the good of his friend. The Abbé de Pradts marvels at his power of renunciation. Because he does not possess this power, the Abbé's subsequent enforced sacrifice of Sandrier is more difficult. The last scene of the play, in which the Superior forces the Abbé to accept the separation, starts with the Abbé's observation that he does not hear Soubrier's voice in the next room reciting with the other boys. It continues with his rebellious, "Always sacrifice! Always the belief that generosity exists only where there is sacrifice!" [22] and concludes with his bitter sobs as the curtain falls. His sacrifice is all the more difficult, since it is in part a punishment for having experienced a human weakness. The Superior is forced to remind him that priesthood is an absolute and perpetual sacrifice, and that he has once again been purified by his acceptance of this sacrifice.

The idea of purification and elevation through sacrifice is the culminating point in the development of Montherlant's heroic ideal. He has created for his protagonists a stature both noble and elevated, which sets them apart from the rest of humanity.

7

The Destiny of the Hero

Montherlant's heroes pursue their destiny in a world apart. Because of their faithful adherence to their ideals and their aristocratic concept of their own worth, they are isolated from common humanity. Everything about them sets them apart, they are misunderstood as much as they disdain. As Montherlant discovered during his travels in North Africa:

> Intelligence isolates. Independence isolates. Candor isolates. Courage isolates . . . There are moments when we feel our difference isolate us as if we were lepers; yes, like a leper in a crowd, having nothing in common with other men except for animal functions, and in every other respect coming into contact with them only through misunderstandings; at a point of isolation that suddenly frightens us.[1]

At moments, some of them may cry out, as does Pasiphaé: "Why should I be different from other people, without having wanted it, without being able to do anything about it? . . . Here I am alone with my acts. I am extraordinarily alone." [2]

While his protagonists are torn at times by the desire to be like others, they cannot. They must always revert to their individuality, for they are indeed different from others. Because of their superior intelligence and lucidity, they share the destiny of the pariah. Montherlant spoke of the solitude of genius in the preface to his *Textes sous une occupation, 1940–1944:*

> Thus, more and more will men of my kind speak a language which the majority cannot understand. Their lonely thoughts rise upwards and do not spread out, just like that thread of smoke which rises in the desert at dusk from the fires of the nomads: that pure, lost thread, thin line between heaven and earth.[3]

There may be found in all of Montherlant's principal characters a secret desire to be misunderstood and hated. This desire, states the author, is a logical consequence of their scorn for the world.

The solitude of the sisters of Port-Royal, exiled from the main body of the Church, was one of the reasons Montherlant felt drawn to them. He stated in his "Theatrical Notes": "In Jansenism I also found exiles, severe, dissident individuals, and a minority; this family has always been, and will never cease to be mine." [4] *Port-Royal* may be described as variations on the theme of exile, for here the isolation is triple: the Order is separated from the Church, Sister Angélique and the other leaders of the resistance from their beloved convent, and, most terrible of all, Sister Angélique is exiled from her faith.

All of Montherlant's heroes are isolated, for they are lost in the infinite solitude of their hearts. There can be neither understanding nor communication between individuals. The kindred soul is a myth, the superior man is alone, face to face with his destiny. In *Va jouer avec cette poussière,* Montherlant remarked that each time he studied the history written about a person who was to become one of the heroes of his plays, he found him surrounded by vast indifference, particularly at the moment of his death. The most terrifying example of this was in the life of Queen Joanna the Mad, which extended over a period of sixty years. In his reading, Montherlant did not find the slightest trace of interest, sympathy, pity, or charity for this wretched creature. The terrible indifference of one person towards another, continued Montherlant, has been experienced by all. The only thing that can be said in favor of indifference is that it usually does not go as far as murder.

Each of Montherlant's dramas embodies the search for human comprehension and demonstrates its impossibility. At times bridges, or rather weak footbridges, are set up from one individual to another, and upon these bridges they may meet for a while. But all of these encounters are merely transitory, since there can be no lasting human relationship. There is only a certain temporary communion within a chosen order of human beings which lifts the individual members out of the ordinary and confers an added grandeur on the members of the group. All of Montherlant's "exiles" long, in their solitude, for the communion achieved by belonging to such a group. This, like the concepts of heroism and grandeur, is aristocratic, for it extols certain hierarchies from which the uninitiated are rigorously excluded.

The idea of a select order of beings was born in Montherlant at the *collège* of Sainte-Croix and has remained with him throughout his life. *La Ville dont le Prince est un enfant* is the culmination of Montherlant's glorification of the "order" of school. The *collège* depicted in this play is both a religious and a chivalric order. The Superior, the headmaster of the school, is the grand master of the order who makes his entrance in the last act to restore the integrity of the order, which has been compromised by all. As a result, he must be pitiless in his reform. Sevrais, although he knows the rules, is an irregular who takes liberties, causing a disruption of discipline. He recognizes that the priests and their students comprise a noble world from which parents must be excluded. Although his mother wants to invite Soubrier home for tea, he refuses because he knows that parents and students belong to two distinct, incompatible worlds. He is impressed with knighthood and wishes to bring its spirit into the school. When he and Soubrier make plans to improve the quality of their friendship, he cries eagerly: "It will be a new life, a sort of brotherhood in arms like in the days of chivalry." [5] The two boys indulge in the ancient chivalrous custom of mixing their blood, swearing that, in their relationship, they will never be guided by selfish motives, but will seek only the welfare of one another. They then intone: *Domine, non nobis,* the motto of the Knights Templar.

Sevrais is so preoccupied with the school that, when he leaves, he wants to have said about him that he did it tremendous good. For the *collège,* which he loved even before he entered it, is his life and his *raison d'être.* Soubrier observes with some jealousy that basically Sevrais is more interested in the school than in his friend. And, at the end, when Sevrais is tricked and expelled, his last words are in defense of the *collège.* Recognizing that he has committed a fault against the discipline of the school, he considers it natural that he be sent away. He, himself, had once stated that were he the Superior of the school, he would not permit private friendships which contradict the spirit of the order. A little boy, whom Sevrais does not know, shakes his hand silently as he walks out of the school for the last time. His gesture represents an attempt to "illuminate this sombre rupture with a light of human kindness." [6]

War is another order, an order of friendship and virility, the continuation of the order of *collège,* where friendships have the same purity as those born in the *collège.* The young Montherlant and certain of his comrades, upon their return from the front, feeling the need for the order, discipline, and virile friendship of the *collège* and of the front, instituted an order of chivalry, "a falling back not upon oneself, but on a handful of chosen beings." [7] After the disintegration of this order, Montherlant turned to sports to find again the "intoxication born from an order." [8] When the bonds of friendship established in the sports arena are broken, there still remains the memory of this order and a feeling of friendship for it.

The religious order presented in *Le Maître de Santiago* is described by Alvaro as a family "by choice and spirit," the only worthwhile type of family, since the "family by blood is accursed." [9] It is also an order of chivalry consisting of certain knights who fought to rid Spain of the Moors in the name of Christianity. This order is now being destroyed, for such superior human relationships, although possible for a while, are ultimately doomed. The Order of Santiago has been in a progressive state of decay, like all other chivalric orders of the time, and its fires burn only in the breast of the Master of Santiago. As soon as the kingdom of Granada had been reconquered from the Moors, King Ferdinand, fearing their power, dissolved them. Now, the few who still belong to these orders are committing the most heinous crimes in their name. Chivalry, whose essence is the defense of the oppressed, is being used to persecute and deceive the Indians in the colonies; its whole purpose has become distorted.

It is for this reason that Alvaro has become alienated from the Order of Santiago. As we have seen, this disaffection is inevitable, for all relationships established by the superior individual lead back to ultimate solitude. The estrangement of the Master of Santiago from the fellow members of his order is but a reflection of what Montherlant, himself, has felt since 1924:

> We counted upon each other, and I thought that when one has known that, it was difficult to lose a taste for it. We ate together, and hope was shared as were the bread

and the wine, as everything was shared. *But, fundamentally, there was something that was not shared.*[10]

Despite his longing for communion within a select group, Montherlant knew that this temporary rapport would lead back to solitude. Wars end and the combatants are scattered as are the students of the *collèges*. The convent of Port-Royal is destroyed and the sisters dispersed. Even the order of nobility through birth, that we find in *Brocéliande*, is tainted. The impossibility of rapport, and the inevitable destruction of all superior relationships, are among the principal elements of a theatrical production which excludes all hope and sympathy and which affirms the sadness of all human things.

The overwhelming pessimism of Montherlant's theater extends even to sensuality which he had always celebrated as the justification of life. In his play *Don Juan* (1958), even physical pleasure has lost its meaning. The seventy-year-old protagonist, the personification of the despair of old age, seeks to escape from the bitterness of life through sensuality. It is no longer the affirmative sensuality of Alban, Costals, and Guiscart that is depicted in this play, but the pursuit of women used merely as the means to forget the horror of the world.

> At my age, my experience of the world fills me with horror, and it is only in the chase and physical possession that I can forget this horror. All around me I find only black night; my hours of love are the stars in this night; they are the only brightness. However, since I do not have a memory, I have said that happiness is written with white ink on white pages.[11]

Don Juan can only alleviate the agony of thinking about his approaching death in amorous pursuit and possession. He is a tragic character, tragic because of his fear of impending death and because he needs the chase and physical possession to prove himself still alive. He states that by his conquests he is constantly offering himself proof that he exists:

> Everything that is not love takes place for me in another world, the world of ghosts. Everything that is not love takes place in a dream for me, and in a hideous dream. Between one hour of love and another hour of love, I pretend to be alive.[12]

He is obsessed with the idea that he will soon cease to exist and can mitigate the pain of this thought only by intense pleasure. He is capable of anything to obtain such pleasures, for he would go mad if anything should escape him before everything escapes him.[13] Don Juan's obsession echoes the confession Montherlant made about himself in his notebooks of 1930–40:

> Sensual desire, the only desire that remains in me. It is what gives me a reason for living. The day on which it is extinguished, there will no longer be anything. Oh yes, I forgot, the desire for death.[14]

In Montherlant's *Eventail de fer* of 1942, we find the precursor of his disabused theatrical heroes in the person of King Khosrau. Using as his source the *Chah Nâmeh* (*The Book of Kings*) of the eleventh-century Persian poet, Firdousi, Montherlant describes this legendary hero who, upon reaching the heights of power, after having received every benefit life can accord to a human being, renounces his power, stating: "I am tired of my army, of my throne, of my crown; I am impatient to leave and my heart is empty."[15] Never, according to Montherlant, was the *proprium quid* of old age better expressed.

How well does this *taedium vitae* of Khosrau prefigure that of Ferrante, who describes himself as a "king of sorrow"?[16] He no longer believes in anything, he has reached the age of indifference, when his successes and failures are all equal to him; all temporal things are passing rapidly before him and abandoning him. He, like Khosrau, is tired of his throne, of his court, and of his people. He is disgusted by the eternal beauty and rebirth of spring, which is always the same. For him, "everything is repetition, refrain, ritornello." [17] Obsessed by the realization that he is soon to die, he sees the illusion and vanity of everything he has ever done and asks why anything he has done should live on, since he ceased to exist long ago.

A hatred for life and a jealousy of youth is evident in Montherlant's men of sorrow. Realizing that they can never recapture their youth, in their frustration they wish to impart to the young their lassitude, to make them despair as they, themselves, do. Words of hope are absent from the vocabulary of Montherlant's protagonists who hate and wish to destroy the future. Inès cannot comprehend the king's hatred of youth and of life and reveals to him that she is carrying a child of his royal blood. The king hears her in horror and exclaims: "A child! Still another child! Will it never end then?" [18] He seeks to destroy her joy by explaining that barriers will grow between her and her child and then, the greatest horror of all, indifference and scorn. Ferrante's murder of Inès is not only the murder of a single individual, but also of her unborn son and of countless generations to follow.

Like the king in his *Chant de Minos*,[19] many of Montherlant's heroes, approaching the end of their lives and still tormented by desires which cannot be satisfied, are tortured by their longing for nothingness. They wish to destroy everything that will live on after them so that they may finally see "a void worthy of a king take the place of matter." [20] There is expressed throughout Montherlant's later works a desire for death, provided that heaven be empty and death lead to nothingness. This desire is a natural outcome of the knowledge of the equivalence of all things, of the fact that virtue carries no more weight than vice. Since everything in life is equal, the original belief that everything is worthwhile, which prompted the zest for life of Montherlant's early works, is transformed into the feeling that nothing is worthwhile, bringing with it despair and a desire for death. "I wonder," asked Montherlant in his notebooks of 1935, "whether the Greeks were not right to consider alternation the equivalent of nothingness." [21]

Georges Carrion wants to die "to stop knowing himself," [22] and Persilès expresses the wish to "sleep a lot, enormously, in order to no longer feel oneself live." [23] Don Juan entreats the commander to kill him "for the love of that God who doesn't exist." [24] Ferrante, too, longs for death, hoping that it will enlighten him and explain to him the mysteries of life. The Chorus, in *La Guerre Civile*, declares that Pompey's death is written on his face,

> he knows it, and if, during his moments of overpowering despondency, he shuts himself up and refuses to have anyone approach him, it is because he is afraid of betraying himself by his voice, which suddenly dies away, his understanding which is stupefied, his features which have become haggard in his swollen face while, with a vague, staring eye, he seems to be looking at death as if he saw it when he looked at himself in the mirror. [25]

Even for Alvaro, who is waiting impatiently for everything to end, God is only the symbol of that supreme aridity, that desert where he may quench his thirst for nothingness and cure his secret anguish. He seeks the void as one seeks repose. Fatigue is the basis of his virtues and, if he claims that action is meaningless, it may be the effect of a desire for absolute perfection, but may equally, without his so suspecting, be merely the symptom of a diminution of energy, of a vital impoverishment. [26]

Montherlant has stated that his own nihilism, if checked at a certain point and marked with the sign of the Cross, would constitute an uncompromising Christian asceticism, but when taken a step further it becomes the atheistic nihilism of Queen Joanna, who expresses Montherlant's philosophy as she reproaches Cisneros for his drive toward temporal power. She tells him that he should have spent his life as she has done, lying on a cot in a cell with his hands folded in a cross. When Cisneros protests that that is death, the Queen replies: "It is the kingdom that is death. It is doing anything that is death." [27]

Most of Montherlant's theatrical heroes are imbued with feelings of indifference and despair and a desire for death. They have arrived at the end of their hope and are indifferent to success, having realized the vanity of struggling for health, power, and money, none of which brings happiness. Montherlant's theater is that of bitter, disillusioned old age. Almost all of his heroes are old men or men who are prematurely old, men who, like Persilès, see nothing but "the abyss behind: a wasted life. The abyss in front: decrepitude and death." [28]

Montherlant has built his philosophy on a base of nihilism; nothing is important, but one must still act as if there were causes worth serving. Despite his recognition of the futility of all human endeavor, his hero must continue to serve, for true grandeur is completely vain. The idea of useless service dominates the works of Montherlant's maturity. It is epitomized by the sand castle children build at the shore, knowing that the evening tide will destroy it. The knowledge of the imminent destruction of their creation does not deter them. Like adults, they are in fact motivated by this destruction because, states Montherlant, "man likes to destroy what he has done or what is important to him." [29]

The dialogue between Inès and Ferrante is the transposition of the eternal dialogue within Montherlant in which one side requires service, while the other recognizes that this service is useless. Ferrante has decreed the death of one of his admirals because he needs guilty men to punish in order to prove his power. He states that one must sacrifice human lives, even when one has ceased to take their guilt seriously, "just like the legendary empty suit of armor which, propped up against the wall, used to strike anyone who passed beneath its iron gauntlet." [30] When Inès asks him incredulously whether one can kill for something in which one does not believe, Ferrante assures her that this happens constantly, and that people also die for causes in which they do not believe, for passions they do not have, and for people they do not love. He acts, he tells her, to make people believe that he still feels something, when, in truth, he no longer feels anything.

All of the heroes of Montherlant's plays fulfill the author's requirements for the ideal man; their blood pushing them towards combat, their intelligence postulating disbelief, making of them at one and the same time the hero and the wise man. [31] They have sufficient lucidity to recognize the vanity of all of their actions and accomplishments. Although they give of themselves, they realize that they have given themselves to nothing, that they have built on drifting sand.

8

Motivations and Passions

Despite their belief in the vanity of all things, and despite their aspirations towards nothingness, Montherlant's heroes are sustained by the knowledge of their own worth and superiority. In a world deprived of all transcendent values, the hero can count only on his own personal merit. This is perhaps the supreme refinement of Montherlant's pessimism, since all the heroes of his theater are victims of their illusions. All of his plays end in defeat because the ideas his protagonists hold of themselves are wrong from the outset.

In an effort to create a realistic and sensitive drama, Montherlant has made all of his protagonists both complex and contradictory. The author has observed that, although conventional theater is based on the consistency of the characters, life shows their true inconsistency.

> Judging a person . . . by one or several of his actions, presupposes that man is cast in a simple mold. However, all of my ideas about man, and everything I have written about him, protest this simplification.[1]

The complexities and contradictions inherent in Montherlant's life and work are most apparent in Malatesta, in whose personality there are a multitude of opposing elements. He passes rapidly from one emotion to another without transition and without apparent logic. He is capable of both the most abject cruelty and the greatest sensitivity. Our first meeting with Malatesta shows him fencing with Sacramoro, his teacher, whom he deceives after calling a halt to the hostilities. While Sacramoro is drinking the wine Malatesta has offered him, he seizes and chokes him, halted only by the remonstrances of one of his servants. Malatesta orders the scarcely breathing body removed from his presence, completely indifferent to whether Sacramoro lives or dies. Later on, the news that Sacramoro has indeed died holds absolutely no interest for him. On the other hand, he is capable of great gentleness and sensitivity toward those he loves.

Malatesta's warlike temperament is out of keeping with his artistic sensitivity. Sigismond is a *condottiere*, a leader of mercenary soldiers hired by the various city states during the fifteenth century. He has always been a formidable warrior, yet, in his adoration of beauty, he states that "all warlike exploits are not worth a beautiful sonnet, or a beautiful speech, or a beautiful maxim." [2] Malatesta's love for his wife does not prevent him from deceiving her constantly, nor does his hatred of naïveté prevent him from being duped and betrayed throughout the play. His son-in-law is in complicity with the Pope to deprive him of Rimini. Porcellio, whose life he once saved and in whom he has the greatest confidence, tricks him into going to Rome to risk his life in his mad attempt to kill the Pope. Then, when Malatesta survives this, Porcellio kills him. It is particularly ironic that the recipient of one of the few worthy deeds performed by Malatesta should be precisely the one who turns against him.

Despite Montherlant's constant emphasis on a heroic ideal, the decisions frequently made by his principal characters, which they attribute to their belief in abstract principles, are actually motivated by their responses to other human beings. In reality, it is often their reaction to certain individuals, rather than a desire to fulfill their ideals, which causes them to act. This idea is summarized by the title of Chapter XV of *Le Songe:* "Everything comes from people." This is particularly evidenced in *L'Exil* where Geneviève, who has chosen a heroic way of life and daily risks her life in dangerous missions to succor the wounded, refuses to allow her own son to enlist in the army. Her devotion to her country is subordinated to her love for her son and her desire for his safety. Jacques de Laprade has stated that Geneviève's action is a fault only in the light of her own principles.[3] Heroism is completely natural to her, her standards are personal and result from a choice. But once she has made this choice, she is unfaithful to herself when she opposes her son's will. This is a sin only because she has created for herself a more demanding morality than that of most human beings, a standard to which she has not been true. Philippe, too, although he speaks of his desire to defend his country in peril, has not even thought of the war until his friend Sénac enlists. Geneviève reminds him that during the months in which the Germans have been at war with France, he has done nothing but play tennis and write poetry.

The Abbé de Pradts believes that he is interested in Soubrier's soul. He declares that to save a child, often all that is necessary is an intelligent man at his side to guide him, a condition that is rarely fulfilled. This rationalization of his interest in Soubrier elicits from the Superior the observation that, although he undoubtedly loved a human soul, he loved it perhaps only "because of its carnal envelope which had charm and grace."[4] The Abbé's moral posture had merely cloaked his unrecognized physical desire.

Although it would seem that Mariana is motivated

purely by religious fervor, in truth she is reacting to her father rather than to God. Montherlant, himself, has stated that Mariana's decision to enter the convent stems from her love for a human being, that her spiritual elevation is merely transitory, and that she will shed many tears after the curtain has fallen.[5] Her love for her father has blinded and hypnotized her and she repeats his words mechanically:

ALVARO   No, rise up higher! Rise up more quickly! Drink [of Paradise] and let it drink of you! Rise even higher!

MARIANA   I am drinking and I am being drunk of, and I know that all is well.

ALVARO   All is well! All is well!

MARIANA   I know that only one thing is necessary, and that is what you said it was.

ALVARO and MARIANA together   Unum, Domine![6]

All of Montherlant's protagonists are motivated by violent passions and intense feelings. Just as they ignore their principles as they react in terms of others rather than of their ideals, so do their excessive passions interfere with the realization of their goals. Both *La Ville dont le Prince est un enfant* and *Fils de personne* are stories of education subverted by passion. Georges, like the Abbé de Pradts, is too passionate to be a successful educator. A good teacher would not have broken with his disciple, as does Georges, but would have been more supple and more understanding. His sudden passionate interest in Gillou, after having run its course, dies as suddenly as it was born.

Ferrante asserts that the Pope is "like other men: he places his passions before his interests."[7] So, too, do Montherlant's characters. Inès sacrifices her life, since she is unwilling to leave her beloved and escape to safety with the Infanta. Malatesta, too, is conspicuously a victim of his passions. Love and hatred follow one another within him with astonishing rapidity. Because he has always subordinated his interests to his passions, he becomes a prisoner in Rome instead of one of the most powerful men in Italy. Excessive passion, as it provokes irrational behavior, is a true deterrent to the accomplishment of the protagonist's ideals for, in the throes of passion, "one can know that an act is worse than useless, even harmful, and commit it all the same." [8]

Montherlant's heroic protagonists become less heroic, more complex, through their faculty of imagining themselves to be other than they are. The author seeks to approximate life in which people are always so different from what they believe themselves to be. The Master of Santiago believes himself to be strong-willed, pursuing without weakness or compromise his lofty and difficult ideal, while making no concessions to the opinions of those surrounding him. Yet he worries about the opinions of the servants as would any bourgeois housewife. This man, for whom supposedly the "one thing that is important, or rather the one thing that is essential, or rather the only thing that is real is what takes place within the soul," [9] is much too concerned with the good repute of his name and with the preservation of the Order of Santiago. He prides himself on his perfection, stating that he is the kind of man all men should be. Yet this supposedly incorruptible soul vacillates suddenly and he succumbs to vanity, the sentiment most unworthy of him. He is saved not by his own strength of character, but by the one he so disdained, his daughter.

Sister Angélique also is not what she had believed herself to be. She hides her extraordinary sensitivity from herself and from the world behind an appearance of curtness and harshness. She coldly declares that "people are contagious in and of themselves. There is nothing like a human affection to cast a shadow on God's sun." [10] Yet she has great affection for her students and for Sister

Françoise. She is capable of descending to the most unworthy recriminations when she reproaches one of the sisters for her treachery to Port-Royal, reminding her that she was received into the community through charity. "Yes," replies the sister, "I was received at Port-Royal through charity. And it is you, Mr. Arnauld's niece, who reproaches me for it! Have we not been told often enough that it is the poorest among us who are the first in God's eyes! You could reproach me for anything else, but not for that. I am ashamed of you, Sister, niece of Mr. Arnauld." [11] Despite the exalted opinion Angélique has of herself, she is the only sister possessed of such overwhelming terror before the imminent persecution that she succumbs to a fear that prevents her from praying and causes a loss of faith in a soul that has disintegrated from fear.

To describe his plays, Montherlant wrote that what is tragic in his theater comes less from situations than from within each character. He added that his heroes are almost all men or women who were strong and who became weak. " 'A theater of weakness?' The word would be attractive, but inexact. A theater of strength and weakness, that is life." [12] It was not only the great reversal of fortune that fell upon Pompey that touched Montherlant, but the fact that there was something within him that provoked this reversal: his flightiness, his emotional nature, his susceptibility to influence, his nervous defect, and his malaria.

Montherlant's characters often react to seemingly unimportant stimuli which act upon a hidden weakness within them. Ferrante condemns Inès to death because of a vain desire to prove himself strong. In the same way, Georges Carrion, who has questioned his continued relationship with his mediocre son, decides to break with Gillou as the result of a blow to his vanity. Although he believes that his only purpose is to make a better person of Gillou, his actual goal is to have Gillou emulate him completely. He is jealous of the rapport between the boy and his mother. In the last act of the play, Georges shows how his pride has been hurt by Gillou's preference for his mother: "I suffered when I heard you laugh too long with her, and stay with her too long, and speak together as if you were always speaking against me." [13] He begs Gillou to tell him the reason for Marie's overwhelming desire to leave the Midi for the dangers of Le Havre, promising to keep the boy with him in Marseilles in exchange for this confidence. Gillou, however, refuses to betray his mother, and Georges feels abandoned. When the boy finally reveals the secret of Marie's lover in Le Havre, Georges murmurs that this confidence has come too late. Since this betrayal surely cannot be construed as a mark of that quality Georges was seeking in his son, we must assume that Georges' "too late" means that he is renouncing Gillou because he can never again be really sure of occupying first place in Gillou's affections.

Although Montherlant's plays, like his other works, are a means used by him to reveal his concepts of heroism and nobility, he has refused to make his characters consistent to effect dramatic unity. The author has stated that he wished to pattern his plays on those of the Ancients, whose tragedies "are those not only of the members of a single family, but also of the different individuals existing within a single being." [14] By showing their complexities and frailties, which make them unable to suit their lives to their principles, he has infused life into characters who otherwise would have remained two dimensional incarnations of his principles.

9

Dramatic Technique

The dramatic technique employed by Montherlant is essentially one designed to bring into relief the psychological development of his characters. For this reason, he has modified material derived from historical sources in certain of his plays. Plot structures are extremely simple, and all external events serve only to effect a profound psychological analysis of the principal characters. This probing into the depths of the human soul is common to all of Montherlant's plays.

In the preface to *Pasiphaé*, Montherlant described the essence of the plot in the following words:

> a human being is faced with an action that is condemned by public opinion of her time and which she wants to perform. She decides to do it. During these moments, what transpires within her? [1]

All conflict is omitted from *Pasiphaé*, which is less a play than a dramatic dialogue between Pasiphaé, who represents unbridled passion, and the Chorus, which is the voice of reason. Before giving herself to the bull, Pasiphaé describes her emotions, which vacillate from pride to shame. At one moment, she expresses belief in the happiness she will derive from her act; at another, the certainty that, when the moment arrives for which she has sacrificed everything, she will feel not a spark of pleasure. Her words permit the Chorus to pass judgment on her passion and to utter sententious maxims to the effect that man unnecessarily creates barriers to his own happiness, that the immutable laws of nature are basically good and logical and should not be contradicted.

Le Maître de Santiago, like *Pasiphaé*, concentrates a maximum of intensity into a minimum of volume. Of all of Montherlant's plays, this is closest to French classical tragedy, not only by reason of the purity and sobriety of the dramatic line, but also because all of the action takes place within the characters. The plot is skeletal and all interest is centered on Don Alvaro Dabo. There is lacking in this play true dramatic conflict which presupposes the matching of approximately equal forces. Alvaro encounters no valid obstacle, for Mariana is merely a shadow of her father. Just as we know that Alvaro will never consent to go to America to enrich himself, so do we know that Mariana, who has always accepted her father's austere way of life, will never permit her father to fall into the trap she has set for him, in collaboration with Don Bernal. There is no one of sufficient strength to challenge Alvaro's will. Consequently, he is free to follow his natural inclinations, to pursue the course of action most in conformity with his desires.

The play is short, lasting only ninety minutes. The action takes place in a single room of Don Alvaro's house within the space of twenty-four hours. The three acts of the play are tightly linked, with no intermissions, and contain no superfluous complications. The single external dramatic act occurs after Mariana's decision to take the veil. Don Alvaro majestically envelops both of them in the great white cloak of the Order of Santiago as they kneel beneath the crucifix, he with his hands joined together and she with her arms forming a cross upon her breast.

Fils de personne is less a play than the portrayal of a

character; the intensity stems from the revelation of the profound inner life of the protagonist. Although Georges' ambivalent feelings toward Gillou are the basis of the play, he has, in truth, rejected him as early as Act I, Scene 3, where he states: "I counted on you. I lost. That, too, was a dream." [2] The spectator is never in doubt regarding the outcome of the play, which is indicated in the title, *No Man's Son*. According to Montherlant, this represents a challenge to the playwright, who is forced to substitute for surprise a penetrating study of characters, passions, and behavior. By reducing the outer framework of his play to a skeleton and leaving nothing but the inner play of emotions, minutely analysed, the author reveals the deepest secrets of the character.

The only external action that takes place in *Celles qu'on prend dans ses bras*, is the arrival of a customer in the third act to purchase an antique armchair from Ravier, a wealthy antique dealer. Montherlant's aim in this play is to depict the progress of an obsessive physical passion in the fifty-eight year old Ravier, who has fallen in love with Christine Villancy, a girl forty years his junior. The playwright has succeeded in capturing all the nuances of this emotion, which causes Ravier to fluctuate between arrogance at the thought of all of his previous amorous conquests, to timidity before the young girl who does not return his love. With the utmost precision, Montherlant shows how an unrequited passion can turn into a feeling approximating hatred.

Ravier constantly occupies the center of the stage. Christine is but a shadow, whose presence is necessary to furnish an object for his passion. The function of Miss Andriot, Ravier's cultured and devoted collaborator, is to permit him to discuss his infatuation. Unlike most of Montherlant's secondary characters, Miss Andriot has a well-defined personality. This sixty-year-old virgin is tortured both by all the tenderness within her, for which she has never found an outlet, as well as by her love for Ravier. She attempts to achieve masculine comradeship with her employer, encouraging his confidences about his sexual adventures, and then suffers from those confidences. At one moment, she is torn by her desire to confess her love to him and, a moment later, tries to hide this love in order to escape his scorn. She is willing to serve as an intermediary between Ravier and Christine, disinterestedly seeking the happiness of the man she loves by throwing Christine into his arms. Then, fearing that Christine may heed her plea, she does not hesitate to betray Ravier by attempting to turn the girl against him. She is pitiful in her attempts to prove to both Ravier and Christine that she, too, has known love. Despite the fact that she seems destined to play an important role, she disappears before the end of the play and has no part in Christine's surrender to Ravier. This is brought about by an arbitrary device which is completely unrelated to the rest of the play. Christine's father is unjustly imprisoned. She begs Ravier to secure his release from prison and, in return, agrees to become his mistress. The introduction of this extraneous incident was necessary to work out a denouement, since it was impossible for the author to do so from the material at hand. The three characters were so firmly entrenched in their respective positions that rapprochement otherwise would have been impossible.

An interesting technique employed by Montherlant in this play to achieve dramatic intensity is the reflection of the identical emotions of the main character in a secondary character. Ravier's passion for Christine is mirrored by Miss Andriot's hopeless love for him, her torment reflects his suffering. In speaking of this play, Montherlant stated:

I show there a man who pursues a woman who rejects him. However, he, himself, rejects another woman who pursues him. The distance among the three people remains the same, just like that between the horses on a carousel, which turn around and around without ever catching up to each other. I could have called this play "The Wooden Horses." [3]

Another dramatic device employed in this play is the revelation toward the end of an intense emotion that has been present, although previously unexpressed. It is only at the end of *Celles qu'on prend dans ses bras* that Ravier's true feelings for Miss Andriot are revealed. While his earlier assertions had indicated affection and esteem for his devoted collaborator, an entirely new light is cast on their relationship in the final act, when he states that he will take great pleasure in destroying her to compensate for seven years of hatred.

There are marked similarities between Montherlant's theater and Greek tragedy, particularly the work of Euripides. We find in most of his plays the same simplicity of action, the shunning of all embellishments in order to present a penetrating analysis of the characters. Montherlant, like the Greek tragedians, does not hesistate to express simple emotions like paternal love, maternal love, and overpowering fear. Georges Carrion, in *Demain il fera jour*, is the embodiment of the classical tragic hero, as defined by Aristotle. He is a prosperous man, not preeminently virtuous, whose misfortune is brought upon him not by vice, but by a frailty. The frailty that destroys him is cowardice.

In Greek tragedy there is always a voice whose function is the moral enlightenment of the audience. This role is played by the Chorus in *Pasiphaé*, which speaks for the author as it comments upon and judges Pasiphaé's passion. Montherlant has stated that his objective in this play was to be both a moralist, who studies passions, and a moralizer, who proposes a certain code of ethics.

There is also a chorus in *La Guerre Civile,* a masculine voice of reason, which comments upon the weaknesses of men. Its moderation of tone brings into relief the strident feminine voice of Civil War, which also speaks from the pit. "I am supreme reason," states the Chorus. "Alone on the mountain, I see things as they are, and I put them in their proper place. I say little, because there would be too much to say." [4] Civil War has much to say, for it is the voice of hysteria, hatred, and murder. "I am the war of . . . prisons and of streets, of neighbor against neighbor, of rival against rival, of friend against friend. I am Civil War, the good war, the one in which people know why they kill and whom they kill: the wolf devours the lamb, but he does not hate it; while the wolf hates his fellow wolf." [5]

Port-Royal was intended by Montherlant to be a model of Greek tragedy, which he described as: "purely and typically static; however, what is expressed there and what is evoked there is much more intense that what is called action in a contemporary play." [6] Although he was a historian, Sainte-Beuve saw the elements of Greek tragedy in the story of Port-Royal as it grew and struggled, only to be deprived of its faithful, then find them and lose them again, and finally be destroyed and reduced to ruins. "This Port-Royal," wrote Sainte-Beuve, "in its destiny, forms an entire drama, a severe and touching drama, in which the ancient unities are observed, and where the Chorus, with its faithful wailing, is not lacking." [7]

In Montherlant's play, the Archbishop Péréfixe acts as the catalyst precipitating the reactions of the sisters of Port-Royal. His intervention provides the conflict necessary to make a dramatic work of this completely inner drama. Aside from the arrival of the Archbishop and his entourage, and the appearance at the end of the play of the twelve sisters of the Visitation Sainte-Marie to replace the exiled sisters of Port-Royal, there is no visible action. The remainder of the play consists of conversations among the identically dressed sisters of Port-Royal. The similarity of appearance, which at first requires strict attention on the part of the spectator to distinguish among them, accentuates their psychological differences as the play progresses. *Port-Royal* has been described by Montherlant as one of those plays from which all extraneous matters are banished, leaving only a detailed psychological exposition. It is the simple unfolding of an episode without plot and devoid of incident.[8]

The playwright has drawn parallels between the dramatic technique in *Le Cardinal d'Espagne* and the technique of bullfighting. He states that the action of this play is patterned after that of the bullfight, and is divided into its three traditional parts. In the first third of the corrida, the bull is erect, holding his head high, proud and suspecting nothing. In the second, he has been checked by the blows of the pics and the bandilleras and by all the charges he has made with lowered head.

Similarly, in the first act of *Le Cardinal d'Espagne*, Cisneros is erect; in the second, he is checked by the queen; in the third, he is destroyed. The entire third act is closely patterned on the third part of the bullfight. Cisneros receives the thrust of the sword, Cardona's insolence, but he remains erect. Dizzied by the insults of the courtiers, he flounders but, like the bull, he rises up again in response to a stronger insult. The matador this time is no longer Cardona, but the king who sends his messengers to put an end to Cisneros.

"In an essay entitled, "Dramaturgy and Tauromachy," Montherlant divides all of his plays into two groups corresponding to the two different schools of bullfighting. The first group may be compared with the "cordouane" or sober, classical school, where the bullfighter rapidly executes a series of "faena" (passes by which he prepares the bull for the stroke of the sword), achieving the maximum effect with the minimum means. These plays are short and stripped bare of any unnecessary effects. His remaining plays are, in his opinion, reminiscent of the "sévillane" or romantic school of bullfighting. These are long, written in four acts or the equivalent, and replete with digressions and embellishments. They remain in the classical tradition by virtue of their psychological preoccupations, but approach the romantic drama in which emphasis is placed on visual spectacle, décor, and local color.[9] In this group may be placed *La Reine morte* and *Malatesta.*

Although primarily a psychological study, *La Reine morte* is a costume piece which, with its division into tableaux, also has visual appeal. Many scenes are included which are incidental to the main action of the play. Principal among these are the love scenes between Inès and Pedro, the meeting of the Infanta and Inès, and the scene of the king presiding over his council of ministers. The general sumptuosity of the play is reminiscent of nineteenth-century romantic drama, differing thus from the extreme simplicity of the majority of Montherlant's plays. Despite the similarities, this play is very different from romantic drama, since the interest of the spectator is focused not on the events taking place before him, but on the psychological study of the protagonist. The line of dramatic action, centering on the question of when and how Ferrante will kill Inès, is unimportant in comparison with the analysis of Ferrante's indecision and hesitations, his inconsistent reactions and inherent contradictions. Ferrante, in his lack of resolution, is Montherlant's Hamlet. Just before dying, he cries out to God:

> In this respite that is left to me, before the saber passes again and crushes me, make it cut this appalling knot of

contradictions within me, so that at least for one instant before ceasing to be, I may finally know what I am.[10]

He then falls dead upon the stage and lies there throughout the impressive silent pageant with which the play ends. The dead Inès is brought in on a stretcher while bells toll. Silently, all, with the exception of Dino del Moro, move away from the body of the king to gather near the body of Inès on the opposite side of the stage. At this moment, Don Pedro appears, sobbing. He throws himself across the stretcher and then takes the royal crown and places it on Inès' abdomen. The guards draw their swords and Pedro forces the assemblage to kneel as he does. While he weeps, they begin to murmur a prayer. The page then rises slowly, crosses the stage to kneel with the others, and leaves the king's body to lie alone on the ground.

Malatesta is unique as it is the only one of Montherlant's plays to start with physical action. The remainder of the play is as full of agitated movement as is the opening scene. The curtain goes up on a bare stage, which remains so for a moment, during which time the audience hears panting and gasping as well as a few incoherent words. Then, in the doorway, part of a man's body appears. Following this, we see two men wrestling, holding short daggers in their hands. They spar, exchanging taunts and provocations, when suddenly one of them, Malatesta, pauses to drink. After having quenched his thirst, he hands the goblet to the other man and, while the latter is drinking, throws himself upon him.

The strict unity of plot found in each of Montherlant's other plays is lacking in *Malatesta*. The first act, which deals with Malatesta's decision to kill the Pope, concentrates on all of the contrasts in the character of the hero. The second act, showing the unsuccessful assassination attempt and the Pope's clemency, is over-long for the subject matter it contains. The third act is completely incidental to the plot, except for the magnificent scene between Isotta and the Pope, in which the former reveals herself to be a master of diplomacy as she persuades the Pope to allow Malatesta to return to Rimini. Porcellio's murder of Malatesta in the fourth act is not the logical outcome of a menace that has been growing from act to act, but occurs as a result of circumstances set up accidentally. There is no accumulation of tension throughout the play, each act starts afresh and develops its own momentum, taking no impetus from the one preceding it.

Although interest is centered on the protagonist, Montherlant here is more interested in creating a spectacle than in depicting a character. Like a Senecan tragedy, the four acts are filled with things to stir the interest and emotion of the spectator. The play is composed of a few highly dramatic incidents joined together by magnificent tableaux which appeal to the eye but have no bearing on the plot. The first four scenes of Act III present such a tableau, in which some sixty courtiers, ladies, and ecclesiastics, all in full dress, are gathered in an immense, luxurious room of the Palazzo Venezia, the Pope's residence in Rome. Soon afterward, many of them press forward onto a balcony. From this vantage point, they observe a celebration, complete with fireworks, which culminates in the Pope's crowning of naked runners with laurel leaves. The magnificence of the scenery and costumes, and the inordinate number of players, make this a superb spectacle which serves to retard, rather than advance the action of the play.

The last scene, in which Porcellio poisons Malatesta, approaches melodrama in its search for dramatic effect. After Porcellio has poured the poison into his wine, Malatesta gradually succumbs to its effects. First, he cries out that he is suffering, tries to get to his feet, and falls back into his armchair. When he tells Porcellio that he is unable to move, the murderer takes up the *Vita Magnifici et Clarissimi Sigismundi de Malatestis* on which he has been working, tears it apart, and throws it into the flames. Malatesta writhes in his chair, howls with rage, bites his fingers, and tears open the doublet on his breast, crying:

> Traitor! Serpent! Ah, I understand, the wine, the poison . . . Villain! My dagger! My sword! The suffering is depriving me of my reason. My hands are covered with sweat. My mouth is drying up.[11]

Then he calls to the great men of antiquity to receive him into their ranks, and once again visual appeal is made by means of the silent pageant which then ensues. First appears the ghost of Pompey, dressed in a toga with his head bared; then comes Julius Caesar, clad in armor with laurel leaves on his head; following him the Gracchi step forward, dressed in tunics and holding one another by the hand; and, finally, Scipio the African arrives in resplendent armor, on his head an immense helmet adorned with plumes. When they refuse to open their arms to him, Malatesta melodramatically announces that he is about to die. As Malatesta lies dead upon the floor, Porcellio continues to burn, one by one, the pages of Malatesta's biography, as the curtain slowly falls.

Despite the visual spectacle and violent action in *Malatesta*, Montherlant's plays, as a whole, may be classified as psychological in orientation. Nature is scarcely mentioned, but when it is, it is used only as a device to perform the specific dramatic function of underlining psychological states. At the beginning of *Pasiphaé*, the Chorus describes springtime in Crete to show how all of nature reflects the physical longings to which the heroine is prey. The evocation of the same season in *La Reine morte* also serves to illustrate the emotions of the characters. For Ferrante, who knows that he is dying, spring, with its eternal promise of new life is a horror, while for Inès, whose eyes are turned toward the future, it symbolizes hope. The rebirth of all things in nature is for her but a reflection of the new life she will soon bring into the world.

The snow in *La Maître de Santiago* symbolizes the coldness and barrenness of Alvaro's soul, its whiteness represents his purity and incorruptibility. In the second act, when Mariana and Don Bernal have agreed upon their scheme to assure Mariana's marriage, the snow stops falling and a ray of sunshine, symbolizing hope for Mariana's happiness, enters the room. But the sunshine is soon obliterated by the clouds and, as the snow begins to fall more heavily than before, Mariana decides to follow her father into a life of sacrifice and renunciation. All of Spain is buried beneath this snow, just as the young girl is to be buried in a covent. The silence of the falling snow evokes the eternal silence to which she is destined.

Scenery, costumes, and all other special effects used in the staging of Montherlant's plays are also intended to emphasize and illustrate the inner states of the protagonists. Perhaps the most effective use of scenery and costuming is to be found in *Port-Royal*. The décor is extremely simple. The stage is bare of furniture except for a few straight-backed chairs. Three doors lead from the set to the interior of the convent, the courtyard, and the chapel. On the left, near the footlights, is the grill of the parlor and, at the back of the stage, there is a small oratory. Within the parlor, the sisters of Port-Royal move and converse, dressed in white robes, each with a scarlet cross on the scapulary. Suddenly, the Archbishop of Paris, dressed in magnificent purple robes, appears in great pomp, together with four other church officials. The five ecclesiastics pause for a moment on the threshold of the room and are caught in a ray of sunshine which suddenly comes through the window into the austere, grey room. The contrast between the rich and luxurious raiment of these men and the simple garb of the sisters, in addition to being theatrically effective, is the external manifestation of the inner contrast between the spirituality and purity of the sisters, and the opportunism and materialism of the ecclesiastics. Similarly, the black garb and black veils covering the faces of the twelve sisters who file into the convent in a silent funereal procession to replace the twelve white garbed sisters who have been expelled, is symbolic of the doubts oppressing Angélique and of the darkness into which her soul has been plunged.

Montherlant disagrees with all theories which classify theater as a separate and distinct art form, subject to specific laws. He states that the dramatist should seek only to serve truth by remaining true to life. For this reason, he protests against the idea that theater must explain everything and defends its right to leave certain questions unanswered. As a result, we never know Egas Coelho's secret reasons for wishing the death of Inès. In much the same fashion, the reasons for the Infanta's excessive interest in Inès are never fully explained. Certain statements made by her, which show a surprising hostility toward men, as well as an inordinate preoccupation with Inès' body, elicit many questions on the part of the spectator which are never resolved.

The inclusion of comic or ridiculous episodes at some of the most tragic moments in his plays is but another way in which Montherlant has tried to approximate life. The uncertainty and fear occasioned in the sisters of Port-Royal by the threat of dispersal, and the spiritual agony of Sister Angélique, contrast vividly with the amusingly naïve gossip and pettiness of certain of the sisters. An amusing episode, treated in the manner of

Molière, shows Sister Julie, red with fever, entering the room crying that she has been cured by a miracle. Sister Flavie retorts that miracles have been overdone at Port-Royal, that Julie is feverish and must be bled again. Julie retorts that she is well and needs the nourishment of a cup of bouillon. The alternating cries of "bouillon" and "bleeding" interrupt the soul searching conversation between Sister Angélique and Sister Françoise.

Bitter, ironic comedy, reminiscent of Shaw, is provided by the Archbishop of Paris. His discussion of his illness, with full details about the number of times he was bled and the medicine he was required to take, together with his furtive taking of his pulse, clashes with the serious nature of his intentions. While Montherlant's depiction of the Archbishop demonstrates his gift for satire, exposing character defects by means of a simple word or gesture, his talent for broad comedy is best shown in *Malatesta*. Following the highly dramatic scene in which the Pope, having guessed Sigismond's murderous intentions, disarms him and reduces him to tears, the two meet privately in the Pope's chambers, where the latter reproaches Malatesta for the many crimes he purportedly has committed.

> Your faults are in the common measure, but your crimes go beyond all measure. You laugh at Christianity. You laugh at Italy. . . . You have betrayed and attempted to poison Sforce, your father-in-law. You are supposed to have strangled your first two wives. You have tortured and killed your old teacher Ugolini de Pili. . . . You slept with your son-in-law, Camerino, when he was an adolescent. You have soiled with your desires the body of the beautiful German girl of Fano after having killed her.[12]

To these terrible accusations, Malatesta, with cynical humor, replies: "Well! Women are made to be loved!"[13] When the Pope mentions an even greater crime perpetrated by Malatesta, the very thought of which causes him to shudder with horror: "you tried to possess your son Robert, who had to seize a dagger to defend himself against you . . . ," Malatesta petulantly asks: "Is it not even possible for family life to have its moments of fantasy?" [14]

Broad comedy, however, must be handled deftly to avoid being forced or vulgar. In *Don Juan*, Montherlant is less successful with his humor. Much of the visual comedy is derived from buckets of dirty water being emptied onto Don Juan's head by housewives as he waits for his amorous rendezvous in a square in Seville. Alcacer begs him to leave the square as the omens are sinister: "A flea has bitten me on the left buttock." "And me on the right buttock," replies Don Juan, "therefore everything is all right." [15]

Alcacer then informs Don Juan that he has arranged a rendezvous for him with the daughter of the proprietor of the Inn of the Three Rabbits:

JUAN   Of the Three Rabbits? For a girl with whom one has an appointment, that's promising. Is she attractive?

ALCACER   When she bends over and her hair falls and hides her face, she's not bad.

JUAN   You fire my imagination. [16]

The humor is of similar quality throughout and reaches its climax in the pseudo-lamentations of the Countess, as she kneels beside the body of her husband, the Commander, whom Juan has just killed:

Amor de mi alma! Is his heart still beating? (She places her hand on the right side of the Commander's chest.) Ah no! I felt the wrong side. (She places her hand on the left side.) Nothing on the right, nothing on the left, he is dead on all sides. Amor de mi alma! I will stab myself on your tomb. I am tearing off my comb from Talavera . . . I am tearing off my admirable fifteenth century shawl, for which I paid three thousand five hundred douros plus one thousand douros for the lining! I am pulling out my hair and I am letting my beard grow! (She throws away her wig as she threw away one by one the other items mentioned).[17]

Brocéliande is, according to the author, a play that conceals profound ideas beneath an amusing exterior. The tragedy of a man ennobled by his illusions and then brought to a tragic end by the destruction of these illusions, underlies the somewhat pathetic humor. In all of the comic scenes in this play, the spectator, sensing the somber undercurrents, is never quite sure whether to laugh. This tragic play, with its gay exterior, reminds Montherlant of an ancient statue of the muse of comedy, which shows Thalia holding the comic mask in her hand, while her own face, with its pouting lips and faraway stare, is heavy with sadness.

Whether tragi-comedy, tragedy, drama or melodrama, all of Montherlant's plays, with their emphasis on the exploration of the inner man, may be included in the broad classification of psychological theater. There is present in each of them a profound character analysis of the protagonist. Although the author has combined the multiple elements of the romantic and classical theater, he has conformed directly to the classical tradition by his probing study of the human soul.

10

Style

In the preface to the revised edition of 1933 of *La Relève du matin*, his first published work, Montherlant criticized its flamboyant language. He added that the stylistic excesses and errors, which had succeeded in making suspect the strong feelings he expressed for the *collège*, were an example of the danger that an inexperienced writer runs in coming under the influence of an artist, in this case D'Annunzio, who however good an artist he may be, is a bad teacher. Montherlant suggested that these pages were as ornate as a Venetian ceiling. Even a year later, added Montherlant, he could have replaced every line of that section by something briefer, more precise, and stronger. He left it intact to serve as a testimony to the style of youth.[1]

With each succeeding work, Montherlant moved in the direction of greater simplicity. Throughout his work, there is a constant balance of classical sobriety and romantic lyricism, of dryness and sensuality, of precision and eloquence. This balance is achieved between the poems of European inspiration in *Les Olympiques*, and the poems of North African inspiration in the first part of *Encore un instant de bonheur*. How simply does the poet express the distress of one whose idol has fallen, in the four lines of the poem "To a retired athlete":

> You were the flower of young men when I
> was a small child.

> Why, after thirteen years, did I have
>   to find myself beside you?
> I turn from you. I speak to you as
>   I look out of the window.
> The trees are dying, but will live
>   again, and the river has not changed.[2]

In poems of a similar nature, the scent of lemons, which are given to the young boys during rest periods, conjures up images of their young, firm bodies; the odor of oranges evokes visions of the chaste Amazons, their female counterparts. The simplicity of language and of imagery differs greatly from the sensuality and grandiose images of nature in poems of African inspiration, like the "Chant de Minos":

> Now, you, freshened in beds of violets, approach.
> I, the King with the thick lashes, who dreams
>   in the undulating desert,
> For you, I am going to break the pact I made
>   with the beasts and with the black spirits
>   who sleep with their necks in the bend
> of my arm, and who sleep without fearing that
>   I may devour them.
> I am not yet surfeited with the springs that
>   gush forth from your palms
> My love for you spins above the shepherd's star.
> Ah! if we could only fly off in an embrace
>   one within the other, like mating flies
> carried off up to the constellations on the
>   giant back of space,
> like the petal of a wild rose carried along
>   on the carapace of a water turtle! [3]

It is in his plays that Montherlant demonstrates most admirably what he had called the two greatest gifts of the writer, observation and imagery. His debt to the literary stylists of the seventeenth century may be observed throughout his dramatic production. French classical style, in the words of André Gide, "tends almost entirely to the use of litotes. It is the art of expressing the most while saying the least. It is an art of decency and modesty. . . . one must always seek the classical author beyond [his words]." [4]

In *La Ville dont le Prince est un enfant*, Montherlant shows his mastery of the art of understatement, as he expresses deep emotion with great economy of means. Although love is the basis of the play, it is as necessary to avoid pronouncing this word as it is to feign indifference toward the object of one's passion, "to harden one's glance or avert one's eyes forcibly from a face, to make one's voice dry, to refrain from trembling when someone comes to sit down next to you." [5] Frequent substitutions are made for "love," the proscribed word. "To take an interest in," or "to show attention to somebody," are used instead. One's love is called a "friendship," an "affection," a "liking," or a "preference."

In *Port-Royal*, too, the art of understatement is developed to perfection. The great tenderness existing between Sister Françoise and Sister Angélique is called a "fondness," or a "small human friendship," or is timidly voiced by Sister Françoise when she asks: "What did I do? I plucked at your habit a little, so that you would turn around." [6] In the same way, involuntary expressions of affection are cut short. When Angélique cries out to Françoise: "I have nourished you for five years with a milk that no mother," she interrupts this effusion immediately with the words: "But I do not know what I was thinking of to tell you that." [7] But all her efforts at constraint are finally useless in the face of their separation and, as is often the case in French classical theater, restraint gives way to a more direct, naked expression of emotion. She is unable to prevent herself from adding: "Now, I am not leaving you; one only leaves what one has stopped loving." [8]

Sevrais, too, is unable to restrain himself for a moment, and calls his enforced separation from Sandrier, "such a wrench." But the Abbé de Pradts calls him to order by reminding him of the words of Talleyrand: "Everything excessive is out of place." [9] And yet, at the end of the play, when the same separation is imposed on him, the Abbé forgets himself and pronounces the fatal words, crying out: "Only death has the right to deprive you of someone you love so." [10] In his torment, he is capable of certain excesses as he sets forth all of the emotions of a passionate heart:

> There is only one thing that counts in this world: the affection you feel for a human being; not what he feels for you, but what you feel for him. Such affection best gives an idea of what heaven must be like.[11]

Yet even such expressions of love are in keeping with the spirit of litotes, since they are surprisingly restrained in view of the circumstances provoking them.

Combined with a certain austerity of style, we find poetic grace in *La Ville dont le Prince est un enfant* in several expressions which blend the simplicity of everyday language with the harmony and beauty of verse. Such harmony is found in Sevrais' complaint that he and Soubrier are always apart:

> Ah! always so close, and inaccessible! I never see you except from a distance, in your yard or in passing, in a corridor; I never see how you spend your life, I who so love your life. . . . There is only one evil, that is absence.[12]

The transformation of colloquial expression into poetry occurs throughout the play. The Abbé de Pradts tells Soubrier: "it is I who am master of your fate. Master of your fate, as I am master of your tears." [13] To justify his behavior to the Superior, he states: "I prayed in my own way: tenderness is also a prayer." [14]

There is a haunting musicality in *Port-Royal*, which has been described as a dramatic elegy. Its biblical style is reminiscent of Racine's *Esther*:

We have removed from our altars the flowers and the draped fabrics and so many trinkets that clutter the other convents, but it is not enough. I would like to be blind, and deaf, and mute, and no longer smell with my nostrils, and no longer touch with my fingers.

I can no longer talk, even now my tongue cleaves to my palate, and the prayers that I would like to offer would not be prayers but cries of anguish.[15]

Montherlant's style not only evokes the poetry of Racine, it also recalls in many other ways the mode of expression of the age of Louis XIV. In *Port-Royal,* he inserted many phrases and discourses borrowed directly from the written accounts left by the members of the Jansenist community. These have been so skillfully intercalated into the play that, without direct reference to the original sources, it is impossible to determine what Montherlant has borrowed and what is his creation.

In his history of the Jansenist movement, Sainte-Beuve reports that Mother Angélique, before her death, said: "Let us go directly to the wellspring that is God." [16] This phrase is repeated by Montherlant's Sister Françoise and then developed into a beautiful image, as she continues: "As for me, I am a tiny droplet that dries up if it is separated from the spring." [17]

Often, Montherlant transposes the words found in the texts to achieve poetic images of greater simplicity and efficacy. Sainte-Beuve records the following words written by Sister Angélique during her captivity:

It seemed to me that I was carrying my soul in my hands, just as a governess carries in her arms a baby who is being weaned, whom she walks and distracts as much as she can to prevent him from remembering his wet nurse.[18]

In Montherlant's play, this becomes:

It is my soul which I seem to carry and to rock to make it forget its suffering, like a child who is being weaned and who is rocked to make him forget his wet nurse.[19]

Maxims abound in Montherlant's work, demonstrating once again his indebtedness to the seventeenth century. Like the moralists of that period, Montherlant excels in such concise expressions of general moral truths. The Infanta's words: "people prefer to die, rather than leave their affairs or take the trouble to put them in order promptly," [20] seem almost to be taken verbatim from Pascal's *Pensées*. Cynical, disabused views on human existence, expressed by many of Montherlant's characters, call to mind La Rochefoucauld:

Each time someone praises me, I smell my tomb.[21]

What is frightening in the death of one's beloved is not his death, but rather how quickly one gets over it.[22]

A life may be filled to overflowing . . . but time can be expanded infinitely to let in someone you love.[23]

The monologues, declamatory speeches, and asides employed throughout Montherlant's plays are contrary to the short sentences and conversational style of most contemporary plays. The author justifies their inclusion by citing their frequency in French classical theater. Montherlant's skillful use of the monologue is demonstrated in the entire second scene of Act III of *Le Maître de Santiago*, in which Mariana delivers a moving soliloquy expressing her love for Jacinto and her hesitations about betraying her father:

Oh my blessing! Oh dearest of all men! You for whom I have retained a bit of my childhood and prepared my heart since the moment of my birth, open your arms to me, take me in my sorrow, and let this sorrow be the last to arise from me alone: may I soon have no other sorrows than yours . . .—But, what is this? A stranger is my refuge, who has never seen me with my hair down, who does not even know my room! And it is from my father that I seek refuge. . . . From my father! He created me, I love him, and it is from him that I flee! (A knocking at

the entrance door . . .) The Count! Oh God! Since it is a
stranger who must find the arguments and the tone of
voice on which my life depends, inspire him to find those
arguments and that tone of voice. It is necessary, I so
desire it. Light upon the things my father notices and
reveal them as he has never seen them. Thus does your
Divine grace work, so do the books say; an imperceptible
nothing, and everything is changed.[24]

Such monologues are frequently found in the plays of
Montherlant, for his protagonists find no one capable of
understanding their confidences. Although Isotta is present in the room, Malatesta speaks only to himself, as he
looks out of the window and sees reflected in all of
nature the expression of his glory:

Great starry night of stars and of fires! Look at the lights
of the city. Wouldn't one say that they were the stern
souls of heroes, who are encamped around me to protect
me? And look at those blazing signs in the heavens, those
stars who, like me, do not sleep. . . . And the sea, do you
hear it? Listen! Listen! It is the sea, the immortal sea
whose sound never changes. Men become tired of hearing
the same words, of repeating the same names. But the sea
on my shores eternally repeats "Malatesta,"—on my
shores full of sweet marble hands and divine sunken
galleys.[25]

The eloquence, at times verging on grandiloquence, of
Malatesta's speech, reveals Montherlant to be a master
of romantic as well as of classical style. André Gide
remarked that the romantic artist, as a result of the
ostentation he brings to his art, "always tends to appear
more moved than he is in reality, so that constantly, in
the case of our romantic authors, the word goes beyond
the emotion and the idea . . . The romantic author
always remains short of his words." [26]

The excesses of language of the Infanta, in *La Reine
morte*, seem almost to have come from a different pen

than the delicately worded conversations between the two friends in *La Ville dont le Prince est un enfant*, where the most simple words are employed to express the most serious and noble sentiments. The Infanta eloquently protests the insult she has received at the hands of Pedro:

> I complain to you, I complain to you, Sire! I complain to you, I complain to God! I walk with a sword plunged into my heart. Each time I move, it tears me apart.[27]

Romantic, too, is the manner in which many of Montherlant's characters externalize their most intimate feelings. There are numerous lyric passages in *La Reine morte*, among them Pedro's love song to Inès:

> Oh beloved head, so well shaped for my hands! Inès, beloved wife, my love with the name "woman," Inès of the clear face, clearer than the words that cradle it, you who are the link which joins me to all beings; yes, all beings attached to you and to you alone, as fruit is attached to the tree.[28]

Inès' expressions of her love for Pedro have caused one of Montherlant's critics to observe that in the lyric tourneys of the courts of love, she would have received the golden laurels.[29] When she speaks to the king about Pedro, she states:

> The day I met him is like the day I was born. That day my heart was carried off to be replaced by a human face. . . . For two years, we have been living in the same dream. Wherever he is, I turn towards him, just as the serpent always turns his head in the direction of the snake charmer. Other women dream about what they do not have; I dream about what I have.[30]

Inès explains that she was born not to fight, but only to love and she describes her nature by means of a comparison:

> When I was a very little girl. . . . if they had opened up
> my chest, love would have flowed forth, like that milky
> substance which flows from certain plants when you break
> their stems. I do not know how to do anything other than
> love. Look at that waterfall, it does not struggle, but
> follows its course. One must let the waters fall.[31]

Demonstrating his stylistic versatility by having each
one's mode of expression reveal her character, Montherlant
passes rapidly from Inès' effusion to the Infanta's
condensed, sharp retort: "The waterfall does not fall: it
hurls itself down." [32]

The imminent birth of her child elicits from Inès one
of the most moving and lyrical passages in all of Montherlant's plays:

> During the day, I do not think about him too much. It is
> at night. He is snug and warm next to my heart, and I
> would like to make myself even warmer to shelter him
> better. Sometimes, he moves, slightly, like a boat on calm
> water, then suddenly a sharper movement hurts me a
> little. In the great silence, I again await his little signal:
> we are accomplices. He knocks, timidly; then I feel myself
> melt with tenderness, because I suddenly had believed
> him dead, he [who] is so fragile. I wish that he never stop
> moving, to spare me those moments of anguish when I
> imagine that he will never move again. And yet, it is those
> minutes that make possible the divine joy of finding him
> alive again.[33]

Inès first describes her unborn son as "a revision, or
rather a second creation of me; as I make him, I remake
myself. I carry him and he carries me." [34] Then, she
visualizes him as he will be in five or six years:

> His name will be Dionis. My little boy with the unbelieva-
> bly long lashes, both beautiful and coarse at the same
> time, as boys are. Always asking you to fight with him, to
> dance with him. Not letting you touch him. Who sighs at
> extreme pleasure. And, if he is not handsome, I will love

him even more to console him and to ask his forgiveness for having wanted him to be other than he is.[35]

Her ecstatic expressions of love for her unborn child contrast with Alvaro's rationalization of his indifference to his daughter, in *La Maître de Santiago*, where he sets forth his arguments with the impassivity of a scientific demonstration:

> If I loved her a little more, I would want to direct her, I would become irritated when it seemed to me that she was on the wrong track or not up to what I expect of her. On the other hand, loving her within reason, I ask nothing of her, reproach her for nothing, we never clash with each other.[36]

The dryness of style of *Le Maître de Santiago*, a dryness underlined by constant references to thirst and to water, "the symbol of purity," is in keeping with the character of Alvaro. So, too, do the expressions of sensuality in *La Reine morte* and *Malatesta* reveal the natures of the characters. Inès' tenderness for her husband and her child is mixed with a sensuality she does not hesitate to express:

> I hold you, I press you against me, and it is he. His neck does not have exactly the same odor as yours, he smells like a child . . . And his breath is that of the doe who has fed on violets. And his little hands are warmer than yours, And his arms are around my neck just like water in the summertime, when you dive into it and it closes around your shoulders, all full of sunshine. And he makes a soft humming sound like a cooing around my neck. . . . Adored child, thanks to whom I am going to be able to love even more.[37]

When she is separated from Pedro, she looks at the sky and cries out for the body of the man she loves. When she is reunited with him, she exclaims passionately: "Let me hold you in my mouth as the savage birds do when they possess each other, rolling in the dust." [38]

While there is an abundance of romantic images in most of Montherlant's plays, there is but a single image in *La Ville dont le Prince est un enfant*, a simile employed by the Abbé de Pradts to deplore the fact that Soubrier does not return his affection: "But you are a small bird: you are always in the act of flying off." [39] The "small bird" helps to set off the more grandiose bird images employed in both *La Reine morte* and *Malatesta*. Ferrante tells his advisors that they should not take to bad faith like fish to water, but should be flagrant in their bad faith, "like an eagle in the sky." [40] Malatesta likens his youthful glory to the splendor of a great bird: "Then my glory was young; it sang and polished its wings in the first morning sunshine." [41] Like a bird of prey, he will triumph over his enemies: "My star is stronger than all other stars. It will devour them like the vulture devours the other birds." [42]

The use of such images, as well as those that suggest great natural phenomena, places Montherlant directly in the Romantic tradition of Rousseau, Chateaubriand, Michelet, and Barrès. Such an image is employed by Ferrante to describe the force of character of the Infanta: "Your exaltation was like that of the wave that swells. With it, you have raised us all." [43] The precipitous movement of the sea is felt in Malatesta's personification of the Adriatic. The repetition of "From me" (A moi), at the beginning of this rhetorical litany, suggests the beating of the waves on the shores of Rimini:

> Take Rimini from me! From me! From me! From me! But the sea which beats against the shores of Rimini, when breaking there repeats the name of Malatesta. Holy sea of Rimini, holy Adriatic, you would engulf my city rather than permit it to be taken by anyone else! [44]

In an onomatopoeic metaphor, the Master of Santiago compares his life and that of his daughter to the movement of two rivers passing separately through underground caverns and merging together to flow into the open, sunlit sea:

> You were following your course alongside of mine in the darkness; I did not even hear you flow. And then, suddenly, our waters mixed and we are now flowing towards the same sea.[45]

The antithesis of light and darkness is found in many other passages, among them the one in which Sister Angélique speaks of her imminent loss of faith: "Even now the wind that blows forth from the Gates [of Darkness] is making the flame of my lamp flicker; what if it should put it out?" [46] Ferrante makes use of the same antithesis to describe his progressive decline into the darkness of death.

> One after the other, things are abandoning me; they are going out, like those candles they extinguish one by one, at regular intervals, on Holy Thursday, during the evening service, to symbolize the successive abandonments by the friends of Christ.[47]

In all of his plays, Montherlant mixes the prosaic and the poetic, the vulgar and noble forms of expression, again showing his penchant for romantic contrasts. The author's most skillful blending of colloquialisms, even vulgarities, with the most beautiful poetic style occurs in those plays that take place in a modern bourgeois décor. In these plays, Montherlant has succeeded in capturing the banalities of daily conversation. The characters generally speak a language in keeping with their station in life. At times, however, they adopt the tone of Montherlant, as does Marie Sandoval, who has been presented as an uneducated, common person, to describe the change which has come about in her life as the result of her decision to live only for her son: "My first life has been dissolved; its residue little by little has been dispersed; all

I have retained in my memory is your childhood." [48] Equally out of keeping with her limited education is the manner in which she expresses her understanding of Gillou's reaction to her excessive displays of affection: "You may even shake with annoyance, when I hug you too hard, to remind me that you are no longer young enough to be my possession." [49]

Georges Carrion's style is consistently elevated. Showing tenderness for his son, he exclaims: "I said to myself: 'He is flowering far from me. I will not have known his blooming. When I see him again, even the form of his laugh will have changed.' " [50] When Marie objects to the fact that Georges speaks to Gillou in a manner beyond his age, Georges states that he expresses himself in a way that comes out of him like fire.

In an essay on Saint-Simon, in *Textes sous une occupation, 1940–1944,* Montherlant wrote that he had the instincts of a master writer and that is why his style has not become dated. He added that Saint-Simon's style is characterized by "a staying-power, a verve, a venomousness, a hypersensitivity, and a sheer pleasure in writing which in themselves would be enough to give it the life that carries a work along until, with an irrestible impetus, it passes through the gates of immortality." [51] For much the same reasons, it is Montherlant's style that will assure the survival of his work, and provide enjoyment even to those readers who are unable to accept his overwhelming pessimism and nihilism.

11

A Song of Death

Montherlant's novel of 1965, *Le Chaos et la Nuit*, carries even further the pessimism and nihilism of his plays. The protagonist of Montherlant's first novel in over twenty years is a Spaniard, Celestino Marcilla, a former anarchist, who has been a refugee in France since the end of the Spanish Civil War. Despite his dreams of former glory and despite his belief in his own superiority, Celestino is but a caricature of the man he once was. In Paris, supported by a modest income from invested capital, the widowed Celestino lives the life of a petit bourgeois, clipping and filing newspaper articles, writing articles that are never published, dreaming dreams of his former military prowess, but taking constant care not to risk deportation by coming to the attention of the French police.

The leitmotif which runs through all of Montherlant's work, the attempt to infuse quality through education and the resultant parental disillusionment, appears in this novel in the relationship between Celestino and his daughter, Pascualita. He adored his daughter before she reached the age of fifteen, but after that her mediocrity came between them.

> Adolescents of both sexes have souls which change as rapidly as does the sky; in the space of a few months they

are transformed, for good or bad; it is almost impossible for those who know them best to predict in what direction they will evolve.[1]

Celestino's refusal to work and thereby increase Pascualita's dowry has contributed to the deterioration of their relationship, but he prefers "politics to money and his disinterestedness to his daughter's welfare." [2] Like the Master of Santiago. he refuses to take the time necessary to arrange for his daughter's marriage. Just as Alvaro sacrificed his daughter to his own needs, so does Celestino sacrifice Pascualita to his political preoccupations. To describe Celestino's sacrifice of his daughter, Montherlant, after fifty years, revises the story he wrote as a child of the young man who throws his bride to the wolves. Here, the young Russian becomes an old Buddhist who lives with his wife in a forest. One day, he encounters an old tiger who is dying of starvation. Seized by pity, the Buddhist gives the tiger his wife to eat.

Celestino's indifference to his daughter becomes hostility to her incurable laughter and her insistence on happiness at any price. Her youth serves only to emphasize the physical and psychological deterioration of old age, "wedged in between the horror of living and the horror of dying." [3] The novel depicts in great detail the loneliness of old age on the threshold of death:

> The days without visits, without mail, without telephone calls became interminable: they gave him the feeling of being dead. He frequently looked at the clock. How slowly did the hands move! What a long stretch of time were five minutes! And yet, formerly, he had told himself that in old age one must be more careful of one's time, because there was so little of it left. But at present, on the contrary, he saw that old age is the period of wasted time. For, since everything had become indifferent to him, what difference did it make what he did with his time or even if he did nothing? And that is why, from morning until night . . . he did meaningless things, waiting until he

could go to bed to escape into sleep. . . . For the first time in his life, he realized that he was on the downward path. . . . Waking up in the morning was the moment of the greatest distress. "Am I really going to wake up? And, if so, how many more times will this miracle happen? And what is the good of this miracle. *For what reason* am I waking?" [4]

In the midst of his torment, a telegram arrives from his brother-in-law in Madrid informing him that his sister has died and that he is to share in her inheritance. His lawyer advises that it is not necessary for him to go to Spain. He can grant power of attorney to someone in Madrid if his political past would make it dangerous for him to return to Spain. However, the telegram has effected a change in Celestino. He regains his former courage and decides to face life once again by returning to his homeland. He is stimulated by the idea of the danger awaiting him, by the "attraction of the abyss." In the same way, states Montherlant, do retired matadors return one day to bullfighting to prove to everyone, and particularly to themselves, that they are still young. For twenty years, Celestino had waited for something to happen. Now, by his own choice, he had chosen the most dangerous course of action, one which gave him back an illusion of youth and distracted him from his approaching death. "He had re-entered the fatherland of courage from which he had been excluded for twenty years." [5]

Celestino, an *afficionado*, is also rejuvenated by the prospect of seeing a bullfight again. In anticipation, he decides to practice the Spanish custom of "car fighting" in the Paris streets. As he flourished his raincoat in the manner of the matador, what was most strange to the onlooker in this astonishing spectacle was that this old man,

whose appearance was rather comical, had retained in these ritual gestures the same grace that good training in

the craft had taught him at the age of twenty. At the age
of sixty-seven, making passes with his gabardine at a small
car, there were moments when, if taken with a slow
motion camera, the spectacle he gave would not have
been unworthy of those spellbinding ballets which are
sometimes performed in their best moments by Beauty
and the Beast, playing with each other in the heart of the
arena encircled with cries.[6]

In this short scene which lasted less than twenty minutes, Celestino "had touched the three limits of his
genius: the Comic, for he had been ridiculous, the
Tragic, for he had risked his life, and the Profound, for
the reasons which led him to risk it." [7]

Celestino sets out for Spain certain that he will be
arrested as soon as he crosses the border. But he enters
Spain unnoticed and discovers that his enemy is only the
indifference of others to his existence. He is as much an
exile among his fellow Spaniards, who accept and profit
by the Franco regime, as he was in France. He had
suffered for twenty years because of the misery of his
country, and sees instead how easily people have adapted
to the ignominious regime of Franco. Here, too, Celestino was mistaken. Only in his apprehensions about his
daughter was he correct. For the first time in her life,
Pascualita feels completely at home, and this in Fascist
Spain. Celestino argues with her and breaks with her in
the name of an ideal in which he has ceased to believe.
He is now completely alone, without friends, country,
beliefs, or daughter. There is only one thing left to him,
the bullfight for which he has longed for twenty years.

Those familiar with Montherlant's passion for bullfighting might expect at this point to again witness the
magical ritual celebrated in *Les Bestiaires*, in which the
sacrifice of the bull will infuse new life into Celestino.
But, unlike Montherlant's earlier works, this is not a
book of life. It is a book of death. "*Aedificabo et Destruam*, I will build and then I will destroy what I have

built," intoned Montherlant in *Service Inutile*. In *Le Chaos et la Nuit*, he destroys the myth of the bullfight, shattering with a devastating blow its pretensions and fraudulence. As Celestino enters the arena, his basic desire, states Montherlant, is to

> profane, dishonor, destroy, trample upon all that he had ever loved; to submerge in a sea of bile his old passion for the bulls as he had already submerged Ruiz, Pineda, his daughter, and, during the last few days, Spain, the revolution. . . . And without doubt, in his political action—in his political philosophy if he had ever really had one— what he had sought to destroy could be compared to the obverse of a medal which is the important side, while what he had sought to construct was only the reverse of the medal. But, at this moment, his need to destroy has another reason: may everything disappear; so that he may leave nothing behind and have nothing to regret.[8]

Celestino discovers, during the course of the shabby bullfight he witnesses, that men come to the bullfight to see done to the bull what they would like to do to their fellow man. When he witnesses the bewildered behavior of the bull upon entering the ring and finding itself surrounded by men who are determined to kill it, Celestino realizes that the bull is man, that it takes upon itself, in a quarter of an hour, all the destiny of mankind. "And men came to see, in respectability and in security, what they would have liked to do to other men. Spain acted out man's passion under cover of the animal's passion, just as the Church claimed to act out the passion of a god under cover of the passion of a man."[9] The bull, at the end of the corrida, is man at the end of his life,

> more and more defiant and more and more duped, more and more wretched and more and more flouted, more impotent and more dangerous at the same time, inescapably doomed to death and yet still capable of killing; such is the bull at the end of his life, and such is man.[10]

In the Preface to *Le Chaos et la Nuit*, Montherlant wrote that the parallel between the destiny of the bull and the destiny of man, both equally uncomprehending victims, was to have been the main theme of the novel. As he wrote, this idea became secondary to the problem of the meaning of life, which besets Celestino after he returns to his room from the bullfight. In V*a jouer avec cette poussière*, Montherlant discusses *Le Chaos et la Nuit* and enumerates the ideas which pass through Celestino's mind as he agonizes in the solitude to which all men are doomed. Celestino devoted his life and risked it for a cause which no longer has meaning at the moment of death. He suffered for nothing, for the chaos of life which will soon dissolve into the night of death. His discovery that nothing exists for him except in relation to himself represents the triumph of individualism and subjectivity. When he ceases to exist, everything will cease to exist with him.

> Neither the fall of Franco, nor the conquest of the world by communism, nor world war, nor the blowing up of the planet by the atomic bomb, nothing was as important as the fact that he was going to die, that there was no hope and that it was imminent. There it was, this thing about which people speak so much, about which he had spoken so much all his life, which he had dealt out indiscriminately without a scruple, and risked without a fear. To cease to be; the most banal, unbelievable, improbable thing. And it exceeded in importance everything that existed in reality and in imagination, it was out of any proportion to anything that existed and anything one could imagine: an incomparable disaster. It had seemed unimportant to him in his youth and in his maturity. Today it assumed a frightening importance, it was the *only* important thing.[11]

Celestino has a hallucination in which Franco appears before him and suddenly is transformed into Stalin.

When he sees that, he realizes the equivalence of all things. What one has done and what one has not done are all the same. This awareness brings with it total indifference, the strongest force existing in the world, "even stronger than hatred." [12] It is because of his discovery of the power of this sentiment that Celestino triumphs over death, strengthened by indifference, he dies undefeated.

Twenty minutes after he dies, killed symbolically by the same four thrusts of the sword by which the bull had been slaughtered that afternoon, the police arrive to arrest Celestino, having finally discovered his dossier in the police files. His daughter, who had sworn to comply with his request for cremation without ceremony, with the trash can as his final resting place, had his funeral service performed in the church of San Isidro. The newspaper announcements stated that he had died after receiving the last sacraments. His body was buried in holy ground and the tombstone bears the inscription: *LAUS DEO*, a final attestation of the futility of everything.

Les Garçons, a novel published in 1969, contains further variations on the theme of death. The novel is composed of two parts: the first, "Au Paradis des enfants," is a reworking of the play *La Ville dont le Prince est un enfant*.[13] Montherlant chose the same theme and expanded it in order to explore it in greater depth. The second part, "Les Opérations mystérieuses," [14] deals with events preceding the opening of the play and those taking place after the curtain has fallen.

While the action of the first part of *Les Garçons* duplicates that of the play, the name of the hero has been changed to Alban de Bricoule in order to place the work within the series of novels on the youth of Alban: the episode of school between those of bullfighting (*Les Bestiaires*) and war (*Le Songe*). This change of name does not alter the fact that *Les Garçons*, despite its locale, is no longer a novel of youth. The center of interest has shifted and the true protagonist is the Abbé de Pradts. It is he who now symbolizes action without faith and it is the story of his life and death that occupies the center of the second part of the novel.

In the preface to *Les Garçons*, Montherlant writes that during a retreat at a monastery in 1929, he learned that the Superior, whose conduct was a source of inspiration to those about him, was a confirmed atheist. An atheistic priest seemed to Montherlant to be a superb literary character and he decided at that time that he would write a novel about such a priest, one whose lack of faith did not prevent him from successfully fulfilling the duties of his office until the day of his death. He would, in addition, reflect the ideas of a writer who was imbued with Christianity, yet who lacked faith.

This priest appears in the guise of the Abbé de Pradts in *Les Garçons*. He had ceased to believe in God when he was sixteen years old.

> His intelligence did not need a God; his heart did not need a God. The supernatural world was as closed to him as that of science, for example, or political economy; for him the natural world was sufficient. According to him, men had invented God because the great majority of them needed one, either intellectually or emotionally; according to him, this need was one of the most common characteristics of human weakness.[15]

He became a priest not to serve God, but to withdraw from the world and to devote himself to his great passion, the education of young boys.

The story of the Abbé de Pradts also includes an account of the painful death of Madame de Bricoule, another in the increasing number of death scenes in Montherlant's work. The physical deterioration of this once beautiful woman is described in detail, as she goes to her grave "to the sounds of the same slow waltzes that had enflamed her youth, and which she heard again on her son's lips." [16] She slept much more than in the past, "as if nature took pity on her; for all her conscious moments were moments of pain: each minute contained a century of pain. . . . And yet, it was this life in which she experienced only physical and moral suffering, it was this life she found it horrible to leave." [17] Before the hideous reality of ceasing to exist, everything becomes reduced to its true perspective. She realizes that she has lavished eighteen years of passionate love on a son who will not even miss her after her death. With this realization, she ceases to love her son and her death becomes a matter of indifference to her since there is no longer anyone for whom she cares to live. She dies, without regret, keeping up appearances to the end for domestics, to whom she is totally indifferent, and a son, for whom she no longer feels anything.

While the death of Madame de Bricoule echoes that of Celestino, the death of the Abbé de Pradts, which fails to convince, seems almost to be Montherlant's version of Pascal's wager. Upon his deathbed, the Abbé is overcome by a great tenderness when he remembers a kiss given to him many years before by the Superior of the *collège*, when he understood that the Abbé did not believe. This recollection, the devotion of the pious old woman who cares for him and who reveres him as a saint, as well as his gratitude toward the Church for having permitted him to lead the life he chose, lead the Abbé to an intellectual conversion. For all of these gifts, he is prepared to make a few "concessions," [18] among them belief in God. His "concession" recalls Celestino's final plea to God, which he rationalizes by stating that, "since God does not exist, it doesn't matter that I invoke his name. . . . Invoking God, who does not exist, is meaningless. But, since everything is meaningless . . ." [19] all actions become equivalent in the chaos called life, before the final nothingness of death.

12

Knights of the Void

The despair occasioned by the recognition of the absurdity of human existence has led writers like Camus and Sartre to propound a new humanism to palliate the anguish of modern man. Montherlant's response, however, is a purely personal code of ethics. Recognizing that there is no reward for man either on this earth or in another life, Montherlant has set up as a *raison d'être* the superior qualities which characterize his hero. His search for an answer to the problem facing the twentieth century of how to live, and for what reasons to live, when all traditional philosophical systems have proved inadequate, has led Montherlant to his concept of the hero. This lucid individual, having rejected all hope of immortal life or of recompense in this life, having realized the vanity of all human things, must still go forward, must accomplish despite the absurdity of man's destiny. Thus, he attempts to make his experiences as intense and as varied as possible. His life becomes a constant wide opposition to the world, instead of a permanent narrow resignation. The Montherlant hero is completely egotistical. Responsible only to himself, he goes forward to meet his destiny, heedless of others. Whatever wrongs he may commit are justified if they serve him in his quest for self-realization. Recognizing that human existence is essentially tragic, the hero cannot content himself with his despair, but must act in order to find deliverance.

While Montherlant's influence as a moralist has waned and may disappear, his survival as a major figure in French letters is assured by his novels and plays. These works remain within the great classical tradition with its emphasis on the inner man, portraying him without hesitation in both his glory and his misery. In his effort to approximate life, Montherlant has allowed his heroes to contradict themselves and to show themselves to be enslaved by their passions, unable to suit their lives to their illusions. He has painted the desperation, sadness, and futility of existing, and the solitude and despair of death, in a language that is remarkable for its stylistic perfection.

In his notebooks covering the years 1958–64, *Va jouer avec cette poussière*, Montherlant reaffirms the principles on which he has built his life and his work. The presence of death is felt throughout these pages as he urgently attempts to transmit to his contemporaries a message that has not varied substantially since his earliest works. "Everything is dust," and nothing has meaning. Nevertheless, one must "play with this dust" out of respect for oneself, acting and perhaps even serving a cause, although knowing that all action is useless.

Notes

Introduction

1. *Nous autres Français.*
2. Justin O'Brien, "*Chaos and Night* by Henry de Montherlant," *New York Times Book Review*, November 8, 1964, p. 66.
3. Henri Peyre, "*The Bachelors* and *Selected Essays* by Henry de Montherlant," *New York Times Book Review*, July 30, 1961, p. 1.

1 – A Song of Life

1. *Les Bestiaires* (1926), *Le Maître de Santiago* (1947), *Don Juan* (1958), *Le Cardinal d'Espagne* (1960), *Le Chaos et la Nuit* (1963).
2. P. 193.
3. P. 31.
4. P. 44.
5. Costals, the hero of *Les Jeunes Filles*, remarks that there is only one way to love women, that is to take them in your arms. The title of one of Montherlant's plays is *Celles qu'on prend dans ses bras* (*Those Men Take in Their Arms*).
6. P. 202.
7. Pp. 159–60.
8. P. 249.
9. *Mors et Vita*, p. 263.
10. *Ibid.*, p. 225.
11. *Les Olympiques*, p. 207.
12. *Ibid.*, p. 89.
13. Reprinted in *Va jouer avec cette poussière*, p. 76.
14. *Les Olympiques*, p. 96.

15. *Ibid.*, p. 97.
16. *Ibid.*, p. 15.
17. *Les Bestiaires*, p. 26.
18. *Ibid.*, pp. 89–90.
19. *Ibid.*, pp. 295–96.
20. *Mors et Vita*, p. 253.

2 – The Hunted Traveler

1. P. 144.
2. *Ibid.*, p. 146.
3. *Aux Fontaines du désir*, pp. 32–35.
4. *Ibid.*, p. 240.
5. *La Nouvelle Revue Française*, No. 165 (June 1, 1927), p. 741.
6. Preface to *Service Inutile*, pp. 145–46.
7. *Ibid.*, pp. 156–57.
8. *Aux Fontaines du désir*, p. 129.
9. *L'Histoire d'amour de "La Rose de Sable,"* p. 72.
10. *Ibid.*, p. 84.

3 – The Novelist

1. P. 167.
2. *Les Célibataires*, p. 7.
3. The models for these men were most likely two bachelor uncles who lived in the house in which Montherlant was raised.
4. *Les Célibataires*, p. 169.
5. *Ibid.*, p. 176.
6. *Ibid.*, p. 179.
7. *Ibid.*, p. 186.
8. *Pitié pour les femmes*, p. 147.
9. P. 322.
10. *Textes sous une occupation, 1940–1944*, p. 261.
11. *Les Jeunes Filles*, pp. 243–44.
12. *Le Démon du bien*, p. 264.
13. *Les Lépreuses*, pp. 164–65.
14. *Ibid.*, p. 168.

4 – A Code of Ethics

1. The threat of civil war made such a profound impres-

sion on Montherlant that, in a note written at that time, he indicated that he would one day write a work on the subject, using as his background ancient Rome where civil war was endemic. He subsequently devoted two novels and a play to the subject: *Le Préfet Spendius*, an unpublished novel centering on the struggle between Christian and Pagan Romans at the beginning of the third century; *Le Chaos et la Nuit* (1963) with a background of the Spanish Civil War; *La Guerre Civile* (1965), a play dealing with the war for supremacy between Pompey and Caesar.

2. P. 294.
3. Pp. 296–97.
4. *Service Inutile*, p. 165.
5. *L'Equinoxe de septembre*, pp. 388–89.
6. *Ibid.*, p. 392.
7. *Le Solstice de juin*, p. 546.
8. *Ibid.*, p. 536.
9. *Ibid.*, p. 467.
10. P. 265.
11. P. 389.

5 – The "Christian Vein"

1. Postface to *Le Maître de Santiago*, p. 659.
2. *La Colline inspirée*, I, 1.
3. Marguerite Lauze and Jeanne Eichelberger, *Deux Mères lisent "La Ville dont le Prince est un enfant"* (Paris: Emmanuel. Grevin et Fils, 1952), p. 37.
4. The doctrines of Cornelius Jansen (1585–1638), Bishop of Ypres, including total depravity, irresistible grace, loss of free will, predestination and limited atonement. This movement achieved a period of influence in France in the seventeenth century. The Church felt impelled to stamp out this movement because of its insistence on predestination, its discouragement of frequent communion for the faithful and its attacks on the laxity of the Jesuits.
5. *Un Voyageur solitaire est un diable*, p. 123.
6. Postface to *Le Maître de Santiago*, p. 660.
7. Act I, Scene 4, p. 611.
8. Act II, Scene 3, pp. 129–30.
9. Act I, Scene 9, p. 463.

10. Michel Mohrt, *Montherlant "homme libre,"* p. 210.

11. Emile Lecerf, *Montherlant ou la guerre permanente,* p. 147.

12. P. 415.

13. Harold Hobson, *The French Theatre of Today* (London: Harrap & Co., Ltd., 1953), p. 192.

6 — The Dramatic Hero

1. The dramatic poem *Pasiphaé* (1926) is a fragment of a longer play, *Les Crétois,* which Montherlant never completed. It is a probing analysis of Pasiphaé's emotions immediately before her union with the bull.

2. Act I, Scene 1, p. 141.

3. Michel Mohrt, *op. cit.,* p. 204.

4. Act III, Scene 6, p. 224.

5. Henry de Montherlant, "Carnaval sacré," *La Table Ronde,* February, 1948, p. 260.

6. *Ibid.*

7. Act II, Scene 8, p. 68.

8. *Aux Fontaines du désir,* p. 39.

9. P. 120.

10. *Les Olympiques,* p. 162.

11. *Procès du héros,* pp. 11-12.

12. Claude Jamet, *Images mêlées de la littérature et du théâtre* (Paris: Editions d l'Elan, 1947), p. 131.

13. *Le Maître de Santiago,* Act I, Scene 4, p. 614.

14. *Carnet XXIX,* pp. 24-25.

15. Pp. 42-43.

16. Act III, Scene 5, p. 214.

17. Jacques de Laprade, Preface to *Théâtre of Montherlant* (Paris: Editions Denoel, 1950), p. xxvii.

18. *Aux Fontaines du désir,* pp. 57-60.

19. *Service Inutile,* p. 226.

20. *Va jouer avec cette poussière,* pp. 118-19.

21. "Lettre à l'Abbé Rivière," *Théâtre,* p. 845.

22. Act III, Scene 7, p. 929.

7 — The Destiny of the Hero

1. *Un Voyageur solitaire est un diable,* p. 149.

2. *Pasiphaé,* pp. 117-19.

3. P. 18.

4. *Théâtre*, p. 664.

5. Act I, Scene 5, p. 872.

6. Act III, Scene 7, p. 917.

7. *Le Solstice de juin*, p. 413.

8. *Le Paradis à l'ombre des épées*, p. 47.

9. Act II, Scene 1, p. 633.

10. *Les Onze devant la porte dorée*, p. 194. Italics mine.

11. *Don Juan*, Act I, Scene 4, p. 98.

12. *Ibid.*, Act II, Scene 4, p. 85.

13. *Ibid.*, Act III, Scene 6, p. 167.

14. *Carnet XXI*, p. 94.

15. P. 90.

16. *La Reine morte*, Act III, Scene 1, p. 205.

17. *Ibid.*, Act II, Scene 3, p. 182.

18. *Ibid.*, Act III, Scene 6, p. 222.

19. A fragment which, together with Pasiphaé, was to form part of the uncompleted play, *Les Crétois*. It is now included among the poems of African inspiration in *Encore un instant de bonheur*.

20. *Encore un instant de bonheur*, p. 385.

21. *Carnet XXX*, p. 385.

22. *Demain il fera jour*, Act III, p. 739.

23. *Brocéliande*, Act III, Scene 2, p. 142.

24. *Don Juan*, Act II, Scene 4, p. 80.

25. Act II, Scene 3, p. 91.

26. Claude Paulus, "Le Maître de Santiago ou l'extase sans Dieu," p. 232.

27. *Le Cardinal d'Espagne*, Act II, Scene 3, pp. 123–25.

28. *Brocéliande*, Act I, Scene 2, p. 39.

29. *Va jouer avec cette poussière*, p. 31.

30. *La Reine morte*, Act III, Scene 6, p. 217.

31. *Le Solstice de juin*, p. 500.

8—Motivations and Passions

1. "Notes de théâtre," *Théâtre*, p. 376.

2. *Malatesta*, Act I, Scene 3, p. 440.

3. *Le Théâtre de Montherlant*, p. 174.

4. *La Ville dont le Prince est un enfant*, Act III, Scene 7, p. 932.

5. "Is the Master of Santiago a Christian?" *Théâtre*, p. 674.
6. *Le Maître de Santiago*, Act III, Scene 5, pp. 656–57.
7. *La Reine morte*, Act II, Scene 3, p. 184.
8. *Ibid.*, Scene 1, p. 168.
9. *Le Maître de Santiago*, Act I, Scene 1, p. 600.
10. *Port-Royal*, p. 994.
11. *Ibid.*, p. 1045.
12. Postface to *La Guerre Civile*, pp. 186–87.
13. *Fils de personne*, Act III, Scene 1, p. 317.
14. "Notes de théâtre," *Théâtre*, p. 1067.

9—Dramatic Technique

1. P. 104.
2. P. 281.
3. "Interview with Janine Delpech," *Les Nouvelles Littéraires*, No. 1111 (December 16, 1949), p. 8.
4. Act I, Scene 4, p. 54.
5. Act I, p. 13.
6. Preface to *Port-Royal*, p. 956.
7. *Port-Royal*, Book I, pp. 24–25.
8. Preface to *Port-Royal*, p. 956.
9. *La Table Ronde*, No. 13 (January, 1949), pp. 33–34.
10. *La Reine morte*, Act III, Scene 8, p. 234.
11. Act IV, Scene 8, p. 535.
12. Act II, Scene 5, p. 475.
13. *Ibid.*
14. *Ibid.*
15. Act I, Scene 1, p. 16.
16. *Ibid.*, p. 28.
17. *Ibid.*, Act II, Scene V, p. 109.

10—Style

1. P. 9.
2. *Les Onze devant la porte dorée*, p. 130.
3. *Encore un instant de bonheur*, p. 386.
4. "Billets à Angèle," *Oeuvres complètes*, XI, 39.
5. Act I, Scene 3, p. 862.
6. P. 993.
7. P. 1049.

8. *Ibid.*

9. *La Ville dont le Prince est un enfant,* Act III, Scene 3, p. 911.

10. *Ibid.,* Scene 7, p. 925.

11. *Ibid.,* p. 926.

12. *Ibid.,* Act I, Scene 4, p. 897.

13. *Ibid.,* Scene 7, p. 902.

14. *Ibid.,* Act III, Scene 7, p. 932.

15. *Port-Royal,* p. 1009.

16. Book V, p. 154.

17. *Port-Royal,* p. 988.

18. Sainte-Beuve, *op. cit.,* Book V, p. 236.

19. *Port-Royal,* p. 999.

20. *La Reine morte,* Act II, Scene 5, p. 194.

21. *Ibid.,* Act I, Scene 2, p. 142.

22. *Ibid.,* Act II, Scene 1, p. 173.

23. *Demain il fera jour,* Act I, Scene 1, pp. 701–2.

24. P. 645.

25. *Malatesta,* Act IV, Scene 7, pp. 525–26.

26. *Op. cit.,* pp. 39–40.

27. *La Reine morte,* Act 1, Scene 1, p. 137.

28. *Ibid.,* Scene 4, pp. 153–54.

29. Robert Kemp, *La Vie du théâtre,* p. 240.

30. *La Reine morte,* Act I, Scene 5, pp. 157–58.

31. *Ibid.,* Act II, Scene 5, pp. 198–99.

32. *Ibid.*

33. *Ibid.,* Act II, Scene 4, pp. 188–89.

34. *Ibid.,* Act III, Scene 6, p. 222.

35. *Ibid.,* pp. 223–24.

36. *Le Maître de Santiago,* Act II, Scene 1, p. 625.

37. *La Reine morte,* Act I, Scene 4, p. 154.

38. *Ibid.,* Act II, Scene 4, p. 188.

39. Act I, Scene 2, p. 858.

40. *La Reine morte,* Act II, Scene 1, p. 167.

41. *Malatesta,* Act I, Scene 3, p. 440.

42. *Ibid.,* Scene 8, p. 459.

43. *La Reine morte,* Act I, Scene 1, p. 141.

44. *Malatesta,* Act II, Scene 4, p. 468.

45. *Le Maître de Santiago,* Act III, Scene 5, p. 652.

46. *Port-Royal*, p. 1009.
47. *La Reine morte*, Act II, Scene 3, p. 182.
48. *Demain il fera jour*, Act II, Scene 1, p. 718.
49. *Ibid.*
50. *Fils de personne*, Act 1, Scene 4, p. 285.
51. *Selected Essays*, translated by John Weightman, p. 237.

11 – A Song of Death

1. P. 56.
2. P. 48.
3. P. 118.
4. Pp. 114–15.
5. P. 163.
6. P. 138.
7. P. 140.
8. P. 234.
9. P. 250.
10. P. 254.
11. P. 267.
12. P. 276.
13. Act III, Scenes 3 and 4 of the play are included in the novel in their entirety.
14. These words, taken from Lacordaire, refer to the mysterious way in which religious conversion is brought about.
15. *Les Garçons*, pp. 98–99.
16. *Ibid.*, p. 300.
17. *Ibid.*, pp. 300–301.
18. *Ibid.*, p. 365.
19. *Le Chaos et la nuit*, pp. 277–78.

Bibliography

Montherlant's works are listed chronologically. Whenever more than one edition is listed, the second is the one referred to in the text. All references to Montherlant's plays, theatrical notes and articles, unless otherwise indicated, are to *Théâtre* (Bibliothèque de la Pléiade). Paris: Gallimard, 1954.

This bibliography does not include anthologies or individual articles by Montherlant. It mentions only a few of the numerous works by Montherlant that appeared solely in limited editions.

Only a few selected critical works and articles on Montherlant are mentioned.

Collected Works

Théâtre (Bibliothèque de la Pléiade). Paris: Gallimard, 1954.
Romans et oeuvres de fiction non théâtrales (Bibliothèque de la Pléiade). Paris: Gallimard, 1959.
Essais (Bibliothèque de la Pléiade). Paris: Gallimard, 1963.

Essays

La Relève du matin (1920). Paris: Gallimard, 1943.
Chant funèbre pour les morts de Verdun (1924). Paris: Gallimard, 1946.
Les Olympiques (*Le Paradis à l'ombre des épées, Les Onze devant la porte dorée* (1924). Paris: Gallimard, 1946.
Aux Fontaines du désir. Paris: Editions Bernard Grasset, 1927.
Mors et Vita (1932). Paris: Gallimard, 1946.
Service Inutile (1935). Paris: Gallimard, 1943.

L'Equinoxe de septembre (1938). Paris: Gallimard, 1943.

Le Solstice de juin (1941). Paris: Gallimard, 1943.

L'Art et la Vie. Paris: Denoël, 1947.

Carnets XXIX à XXXV (February 19, 1935 to January 11, 1939). Paris: La Table Ronde, 1947.

Carnets XLII à XLIII (January 1, 1942 to December 31, 1943). Paris: La Table Ronde, 1948.

Textes sous une occupation, 1940–1944. Paris: Gallimard, 1953.

Carnets XXII à XXVIII (April 23, 1932 to November 22, 1934). Paris: La Table Ronde, 1955.

Un Voyageur solitaire est un diable. Monaco: Editions du Rocher, 1955.

Carnets (Années 1930 à 1944). Paris: Gallimard, 1957.

Va jouer avec cette poussière (Carnets 1958–64). Paris: Gallimard, 1966.

Discours de réception de M. Henry de Montherlant à l'Académie Française et réponse de M. le Duc de Lévis Mirepoix. Paris: Gallimard, 1963.

Autobiographical Works of Fiction and Novels

Le Songe (1922). Paris: Gallimard, 1954.

Les Bestiaires (1926). Paris: Gallimard, 1954.

La Petite Infante de Castille. Paris: Grasset, 1929.

La Rose de Sable (1930). Paris: Gallimard, 1968.

Les Célibataires (1934). Paris: Fayard, 1934.

Les Jeunes Filles (1936). Paris: Gallimard, 1954.

Pitié pour les Femmes (1936). Paris: Gallimard, 1954.

Le Démon du Bien (1937). Paris: Gallimard, 1954.

Les Lépreuses (1939). Paris: Gallimard, 1954.

L'Histoire d'amour de "La Rose de Sable." Paris: Plon, 1954.

Le Chaos et la Nuit. Paris: Gallimard, 1963.

Les Garçons. Paris: Gallimard, 1969.

Plays

L'Exil, 1929.

Pasiphaé, 1936.

La Reine morte, 1942.

Fils de personne, 1943.
Un Incompris, 1943.
Fils des autres, Un Incompris, Fils de personne. Paris: Gallimard, 1944.
Malatesta, 1946.
Le Maître de Santiago, 1947.
Demain il fera jour, 1949.
Celles qu'on prend dans ses bras, 1950.
La Ville dont le Prince est un enfant, 1951.
Port-Royal, 1954.
Brocéliande. Paris: Gallimard, 1956.
Don Juan. Paris: Gallimard, 1958.
Le Cardinal d'Espagne. Paris: Gallimard, 1960.
La Guerre Civile. Paris: Gallimard, 1965.

Poetry

Encore un instant de bonheur (1934). Paris: Gallimard, 1946.

Selected Works in Limited Editions

Hispano-Moresque. Paris: Emile-Paul, 1929.
Pour une Vierge noire. Paris: Les Editions du Cadran, 1930.
Il y a encore des paradis (*Images d'Alger*). Alger: Soubiron, 1935.
La Possession de soi-même. Paris: Flammarion, 1938.
Sur les femmes. Marseille: Editions du Sagittaire, 1942.
L'Eventail de fer. Paris: Flammarion, 1944.
Saint-Simon. Paris: L'Originale, 1948.
Coups de soleil—Afrique—Andalousie. Paris: La Palatine, 1950.
España Sagrada. Paris: Dominique Wapler, 1951.
Le Fichier Parisien. Paris: Plon, 1952.

English Translations of Montherlant's Works

Le Songe—The Dream. Trans. by Terence Kilmartin. London: Weidenfeld & Nicolson, 1962.
Les Bestiaires—The Matador. Trans. by Peter Wiles. London: Elek, 1957.

Les Célibataires—The Bachelors. Trans. by Terence Kilmartin. London: Weidenfeld & Nicolson, 1960.

Les Jeunes Filles—The Young Girls. Trans. by Thomas McGreevy. London: Routledge, 1937.

Pitié pour les Femmes—Pity for Women. Trans. by John Rodker. London: Routledge, 1937.

Le Démon du Bien—The Demon of Good. Trans. by John Rodker. London: Routledge, 1937.

Les Lépreuses—The Lepers. Trans. by John Rodker. London: Routledge, 1940.

(*The Young Girls* and *Pity for Women* are published together under the title: *Pity for Women; The Demon of Good* and *The Lepers* under the title: *Costals and the Hippogriff*).

L'Histoire d'amour de "La Rose de Sable"—Desert Love. Trans. by Alec Brown. London: Elek, 1957.

Le Chaos et la Nuit—Chaos and Night. Trans. by Terence Kilmartin. London: Weidenfeld & Nicolson, 1964.

Selected Essays. Trans. by John Weightman. London: Weidenfeld & Nicolson, 1960.

La Reine morte (*Queen after Death*), *Fils de personne* (*No Man's Son, Malatesta, Le Maître de Santiago* (*The Master of Santiago*), *Demain il fera jour* (*Tomorrow the Dawn*), in *The Master of Santiago and Four Other Plays*. Trans. by Jonathan Griffin. New York: Knopf, 1951.

Selected Critical Works and Articles on Montherlant

Alheinc, Raoul. "Montherlant et le bovarysme," *La Table Ronde*, No. 103–4 (July–August, 1956), pp. 208–15.

Becker, Lucille. "Pessimism and Nihilism in the Plays of Henry de Montherlant," *Yale French Studies*, No. 29 (Spring–Summer, 1962), pp. 88–91.

Becker, Lucille and della Fazia, Alba. *Le Maître de Santiago*. Edited with Introduction, Notes and Vocabulary. Boston: D. C. Heath & Co., 1965

Beer, Jean de. *Montherlant, ou l'homme encombré de Dieu*. Paris: Flammarion, 1963.

Beigbeder, Marc. "Montherlant ou le roman perpétuel" (Problèmes du roman sous la direction de Jean Prévost), *Confluences*, Nos. 21–24 (1943), pp. 78–83.

Bodart, Roger. *Montherlant ou l'armure vide.* Liége: La Sixaine, 1946.

Bordonave, Georges. *Henry de Montherlant.* Paris: Editions Universitaires, 1954.

Breuzière, Maurice. "Portée morale et humaine du théâtre de Montherlant," *Le Théâtre contemporain* (Recherches et débats, Nouvelle série, Cahier No. 2). Paris: Librairie Arthème Fayard, October 1952, pp. 169–82.

Brulard, Roger. *Montherlant et ses masques.* Brussels: Editions "La Lecture au Foyer," 1953.

Cruickshank, John. *Montherlant.* London: Oliver & Boyd, Ltd., 1964.

Datain, Jean. *Montherlant et l'héritage de la Renaissance.* Paris: Amiot Dumont, 1956.

Debrie-Panel, Nicole. *Montherlant: l'art et l'amour.* Lyon: Vitte, 1960.

Eichelberger, Jeanne and Lauze, Marguerite. *Deux Mères lisent "La Ville dont le Prince est un enfant."* Paris: Emmanuel Grevin et Fils, 1952.

Faure-Biguet, J. N. *Les Enfances de Montherlant,* suivi de *Montherlant, homme de la Renaissance.* Paris: Henri Lefebvre, 1948.

Laprade, Jacques de. *Le Théâtre de Montherlant.* Paris: Editions Denoel, 1950.

Lanteri-Laura, Georges. "Compréhension et solitude dans le théâtre de Montherlant," *Etudes Philosophiques*, No. 2–3 (April–September, 1950), pp. 200–201.

Lecerf, Emile. *Montherlant ou la guerre permanente.* Brussels: Editions de la Toison d'Or, 1944.

Marissel, André. *Montherlant.* Paris: Editions Universitaires (Collection "Classiques du XXème siècle"), 1966.

Mériel, E.-H. *Henry de Montherlant.* Paris: Editions de la Nouvelle Revue Critique, 1936.

Mohrt, Michel. *Montherlant "homme libre."* Paris: Gallimard, 1943.

Paulus, Claude. "Le Maître de Santiago ou l'extase sans Dieu," *Synthèses*, No. 56 (January, 1951), pp. 226–38.

Perruchot, Henri. *Montherlant*. Paris: Gallimard, 1959.

Saint-Pierre, Michel de. *Montherlant, bourreau de soi-même*. Paris: Gallimard, 1949.

Sandelion, Jeanne. *Montherlant et les femmes*. Paris: Plon, 1950.

Sipriot, Pierre. *Montherlant par lui-même*. Paris: Editions du Seuil (Collection "Ecrivains de toujours"), 1953.

Sipriot, Pierre, ed. *La Table Ronde*. Special edition on Montherlant, No. 155. Paris: Librairie Plon, November 1960. (Containing articles by Michel Mohrt, Henri Massis, Georges Bordonave, Léon-Pierre Quint, Henri Clouard, etc.).

Thierry, Jean Jacques, ed. *Montherlant vu par des jeunes de 17 à 27 ans* (Containing articles by Marc Alias, Lucille Becker, André Burguière, Martine Cadieu, etc.). Paris: La Table Ronde, 1959.

Selected Works Containing Studies of Montherlant

Albérès. R.-M. *L'Aventure intellectuelle au 20ème siècle*. Paris: La Nouvelle Edition, 1950.

Arland, Marcel. *La Grâce d'Ecrire*. Paris: Gallimard, 1955.

Barjon, Louis. *Mondes d'écrivains, Destinées d'hommes*. Paris: Tournai, 1960.

Beauvoir, Simone de. *Le Deuxième sexe*. Paris: Gallimard, 1949.

Bendz, Ernst. *Visages d'écrivains*. Paris: Les Presses de la Cité, 1948.

Boisdeffre, Pierre. *Métamorphose de la littérature de Barrès à Malraux*. Paris: Editions Alsatis, 1950.

————. *Une Histoire vivante de la littérature d'aujourd'hui*. Paris: Librairie Académique Perrin, 1964.

Brodin, Pierre. *Présences contemporaines*. Paris: Editions Debresse, 1954.

Burnet, Etienne. *Essences*. Paris: Editions Scheur, 1929.

Castay, Marcel. *Les Héritiers de la couronne*. Paris: Librairie des Lettres, 1952.

Chaigne, Louis. *Vie et oeuvres d'écrivains*, 3° série, Vol. III. Paris: Lanore, 1950.

Gassner, John. *Masters of the Drama*, 3rd ed. New York: Dover Publications, 1954.

Hobson, Harold. *The French Theater of Today, An English View*. London: Harrap & Co., Ltd., 1953.

Jaccard, Pierre. *Trois Contemporains*. Lausanne: Eds. de la Concorde, 1945.

Jamet, Claude. *Images mêlées de la littérature et du théâtre*. Paris: Editions de l'Elan, 1947.

———. *Images de la littérature*. Paris: Fernand Sorlot, 1943.

Kemp, Robert. *La Vie des livres*. Paris: Albin Michel, 1955.

———. *La Vie du théâtre*. Paris: Albin Michel, 1956.

Mauriac, Pierre. *L'Ecrivain et l'événement*. Paris: Editions Silsé, 1947.

Perruchot, Henri. *La Haine des masques*. Paris: La Table Ronde, 1955.

Picon, Gaëtan. *Panorama de la nouvelle littérature*. Paris: Gallimard, 1949.

Poulet, Robert. *La Lanterne Magique*. Vol. I. Paris: Nouvelles Editions Debresse, 1956.

Simon, Pierre-Henri. *Procès du héros*. Paris: Editions du Seuil, 1950.

———. *Témoins de l'homme*. Paris: Armand Colin, 1951.

Index